METAPHYSICAL REALITIES IN PSYCHOLOGY AND MANAGEMENT

About the Author

M.B. Sharan, Ph.D. (Patna University) is Ex-Professor & Head, Department of Humanities & Social Sciences, IIT, Kharagpur where he taught psychology and management courses to undergraduate and postgraduate students for more than thirty years. Prior to this, he was a Lecturer in Psychology in Patna and Bhagalpur Universities. After retirement from IIT service in 2005, he served as Dean (Academic) and Principal at RIMS, Rourkela and as Emeritus Professor at PIET, Rourkela till 2009. He has authored/edited three books: *Management Through Interpersonal Relationships*, *Psychology Matters: Development, Health and Organization*, and *A Study of Role Conflict and its Influence on Role Performance* and has published a good number of articles in national and international journals. He was the President of the National Academy of Psychology for the year 2006-07. His biography figures in 8th edition of "Who's Who in the World."

Metaphysical Realities in Psychology and Management

A Sacred Path to Intuitive Awareness

By
M.B. Sharan, *Ph.D.*

Foreword by
Henry Reed

CONCEPT PUBLISHING COMPANY PVT. LTD.
NEW DELHI-110059

ISBN-13: 978-81-8069-756-2

First Published 2011

Published and Printed by

Concept Publishing Company Pvt. Ltd.
Regd. Office:
A/15-16, Commercial Block, Mohan Garden
New Delhi-110059 (India)
Phones : 25351460, 25351794, *Fax* : 091-11-25357109
Email : publishing@conceptpub.com,
Website: www.conceptpub.com

Editorial Office:
H-13, Bali Nagar, New Delhi-110 015, India.

Cataloging in Publication Data--*Courtesy:* D.K. Agencies (P) Ltd. <docinfo@dkagencies.com>

Sharan, M. B. (Mithila Bihari), 1943-

Metaphysical realities in psychology and management : a sacred path to intuitive awareness/ by M.B. Sharma ; foreword by Henry Reed.

p. cm.

Includes bibliographical references and index.

ISBN 9788180697562

1. Psychology. 2. Management. 3. Metaphysics. I. Title.

DDC 150 22

Dedicated

to

My Soul Mate

Savita Sharan

For Showing Me

The Path of Intuitive Awareness

Foreword

Mathematics, the Queen of the Sciences, is primarily a mental activity, drawing upon both rationality and intuition. One of the advantages of mathematics is the freedom mathematicians enjoy to explore the implications of impossible ideas. Mathematicians are free to begin with assumptions, or axioms, statements that cannot be proven, yet which prove to be very provocative by way of insights to which they lead.

What passes for science as the twentieth century turns into the twenty first is based upon an axiom, an assumption, but unlike mathematics, it is one that is rarely put up for examination. The assumption is that reality is comprised entirely of matter, or of things and events which are observable by sensory apparatus. The results of persuing the implications of this assumption have been enormous, leading to major technological advances. Yet none of this scientific progress has led to any clues to such questions as "What is the purpose of a human life?" Instead, our technologically advanced science has led to our humanity's facing an out of control, clockwork universe, ticking, without meaning, towards its eventual, prewritten destiny.

Science, as a form of human collaboration, arose distinct from another form of human collaboration, religious devotion. In the latter, all truths arose from the King/Priest. At the time of Copernicus, that King/Priest was the Catholic Pope. Truth emanated from the lips of the Pope, who had the sole authority to interpret the book of truth, the Bible. Truth was something passed down, authoritatively, from traditional sources. Science, on the other hand, was born of a democratic spirit, from the natural tendency of humans to want to share and compare their experiences. As a human enterprise, science proclaimed that truth was best discovered by direct experience and the comparing of that experience by independent observers. It took a while, but gradually the idea of sharing and comparing experiences was reduced to comparing quantitative measurements of material objects. What was an expediency to facilitate comparison became an unclaimed axiom of science: what is real is what is made of matter?

Now let's suppose we took as a starting axiom, "what is real is what makes a difference in a person's life." Let's use that as a basis for sharing and comparing experiences. In other words, let's use that axiom as a basis for beginning our scientific explorations. To do so has major implications for what truths we may uncover. For example, it has been proven to the satisfaction of most logical, materialistically oriented minds that a proof of God's existence is not possible. Yet, if we use our novel axiom, we can say, without doubt, that the idea of God is a reality for many people and makes a tremendous difference in their lives.

Alongside the materialistic tradition of science there exists another thread of the history of human collaboration. It concerns the methods, observations, and interpretations in the area of spirituality. For countless centuries there have been those individuals whose research has been of a more inward, intuitive nature. Many have written of their experiences. Others have studied these accounts and shown the commonalities and agreements existing among these "subjective" explorations. There is an empiricism of the mind, of inner experience.

Different axioms spur different modes of exploration. To take an important example. Is the Universe comprised of separate things that impact upon one another in time and space? Or is the Universe a creature of a meaningful "here and now" eternity of unfolding awareness? It depends upon how one looks, or, in other words, the tools of observation that are employed. In a series of experiments, I compared what participants experienced when sitting facing one another. I directed them to use their eyes to look and examine each other. I also asked them to close their eyes, enter into the experience of their hearts, and "feel" the other person. These two modalities of observation resulted in two very different sets of data. In the first, participants could describe the appearance of each other. In the second, they were able to share some empathy for the subjective experience of the other. When they used their eyes, they saw that they were separate. When they used their imagination, they felt as if they were "one," and experienced empathy. I found that during their silent, "imaginary" conversations, they experienced such subjective events as images, feelings and memories, but which later corresponded to experiences of the other participant. There was a certain "objective," or consensus reality to their shared subjectivity (you can download reprints of this two-part study at http://henryreed.com/close2you1.pdfand and http://henryreed.com/close2you2.pdf).

How is it that mathematicians, working purely intuitively within the subjectivity of their own minds can develop mathematical systems that later prove to be perfectly analogous to patterns in material nature? How is it that Edgar Cayce, who was relatively uneducated, could, from a deep intuitive trance, describe the molecular activities in the human body that provided the link between mental events and hormonal ones, processes that took decades of later medical research to discover and confirm his insights? May we infer that the same "creatively intelligent designs" form both the elements found in the mind and the elements found in the material world? If so, then by using the powers of the imagination to "perceive" realities that do not have an observable materialistic counterpart, we might scientifically proceed to understand some mysteries that traditional science has ignored. The current volume of extraordinary work proves that it is so. A dawn of a new era in science is upon us, and here it takes great inspiration from one of the oldest endeavours of human exploration known to history, the creative work of Vedanta, the ancient spiritual science of India.

Henry Reed, Ph.D.
Professor of Transpersonal Studies, Atlantic University
Director, Edgar Cayce Institute for Intuitive Studies.

Acknowledgements

The whole of my academic life of teaching and research in psychology and management has led to this book. I am, therefore, grateful to all my teachers in general and to Late Prof. S.M. Mohsin (Ex-Professor & Head, Department of Psychology, Patna University, Patna), Late Prof. A.K. Sinha (Ex-Professor & Head, Department of Psychology, Bihar University, Muzaffarpur), and Prof. K.C. Sahu (Ex-Professor & Head, Department of Industrial Engineering & Management, IIT, Kharagpur) in particular for making me an academician. Directly or indirectly, they have taught me a lot and have made me whatsoever I am today. In this journey, there are many other persons—authors, researchers, colleagues, family members, friends, and students—who have also helped me in learning many more things. I express my sincere thanks to each one of them.

When I started my career as a teacher of Psychology in 1965, I was excited to teach more and more about "scientific" psychology. But gradually, I found applied psychology to be more useful than the scientific one. As a result, I decided to teach industrial psychology and some management courses. While teaching these subjects, I realized the importance of interpersonal relationships, interpersonal communication, and personal spirituality. This really changed my personality and my behaviour with others. In this process, a time came when I got convinced that any phenomenon could be explained partly scientifically and partly spiritually. Since then, I have been trying my best to understand the "mystery" of spirituality. Perhaps, this is the reason why today I am talking more and more about Integral Psychology and New Age Spirituality. This book, *"Metaphysical Realities in Psychology and Management"* is the result of this kind of realization and experience. In this spiritual development, Association for Research and Enlightenment (A.R.E.), founded by Edgar Cayce, has inspired me the most for writing good papers on topics related to spirituality and getting them published in its online magazine, *The Intuitive-Connections Network.* I am really indebted to this Association in general and to Dr. Henry Reed (Editor) in particular for all these.

I consider myself to be a silent worker. If I am known to others in psychology, management and spirituality, I shall like to give this credit to my students in general and to the Members of the National Academy of Psychology (NAOP), India in particular for electing me as its President for the year 2006-07. I really felt elevated and honoured because this brought me in the limelight. For this, I shall remain grateful to this NAOP for ever.

When I look back, I find there are some other persons who have also helped me in various ways. It is not possible for me to name here everyone. However, I would like to mention the names of at least two persons—Dr. Deepa Chatterjee (Senior Lecturer, RIMS, Rourkela) for going through all the articles selected for this book and suggesting corrections and Mrs. Padmini Barik (Lecturer, PIET, Rourkela) for setting the materials for publication. I express my sincere thanks to all these persons.

Contents

Introduction

What is Metaphysics?

Metaphysics is a New Movement of the Spirit which stands for the deeper realities of the Universe, the things which are eternal, and the things which are above and beyond the outer and phenomenal realm. This New Movement concerns itself with the Absolute Truth, especially with the practical application of that Absolute Truth of Being in all the affairs of our daily lives. It emphasizes God as the only one Absolute Reality. As defined by Funk and Wagnall's Standard College Dictionary, Metaphysics is "the branch of philosophy that investigates principles of reality transcending those of any particular science, traditionally including cosmology, ontology, and speculative philosophy."

Traditionally, the word "Metaphysics" was used as over and beyond physics by the followers of Aristotle because it came from ancient Greece, where it was a combination of two words—"Meta" (meaning over and beyond) and "Physics" (meaning physical). But in philosophy, it acquired a far profound meaning—the science of real being—which is now also well accepted in other subjects. Thinkers interested in religion, parapsychology, mysticism, yoga, extra-sensory perception, dream, Jungian psychology, astrology, meditation, self-help study, positive thinking, reincarnation, etc. are all coming together to support this movement as a "Spiritual Philosophy of Life." As a result, these Metaphysical Practitioners, irrespective of their specializations and backgrounds, are actively engaged today in teaching this spiritual philosophy which aims at finding the ultimate reality and the purpose of human life. In USA, there are some Universities like Atlantic University, University of Metaphysics, and University of Sedona which are exclusively teaching this subject and giving Masters and Doctoral degrees.

Physical and Metaphysical Realities

There is no sure way to know how many realities are there in the Universe. Reality is so complex that no science or religion perhaps can determine its exact number. However, at the very least, it has to be two: physical and metaphysical. Physical is related to mass or matter, and metaphysical is related to energy or thought. In many cases, particularly in the case of cause and effect relationship, the physical is visible whereas the metaphysical is invisible. Scientists have been very successful in dealing with certain components of the physical reality. But they have kept their "hands off" from the metaphysical reality as they have not found any "scientific" proof for that. Realizing the inadequacy of science, religion has come forward to tell us something about the metaphysical realities like God and human soul. All such information, however, are completely based on faith and belief. Throughout history, people have believed in God, and have experienced Him in some way. Today, some are even successful in collecting evidences, such as anthropic cosmological evidence, which empirically suggest the existence of God. Similarly, many of us believe in Universal or Superconscious Mind, Collective Unconscious Mind, Higher

Self, Prayer, Meditation, Miracles, *Karma* and Reincarnation, and so on. Can Scientists say that all these persons are doing something wrong? Is it not a fact that many of the great scientists like Newton, Galileo, Einstein, Darwin also believed in God? If this is the case, then why not we change our mindset and conclude that "validation of all forms of reality cannot be limited to only scientific or purely mathematical methods of proofs?" Some other convincing methods should also be accepted to validate reality. Once we change our mindset in this line, we shall find that in every subject there are many things which can be explored as metaphysical realities. Perhaps, this is the reason why today a good number of open-minded professors, scientists, and physicians are coming together on the same platform to welcome spiritual masters because they know that they have the correct answers to various problems.

So far number is concerned, yes; the number of ultimate reality is only one—*Spirit.* Buddhism and Hinduism say very clearly that the physical world is simply a mass illusion (*samsara* or *maya*). Scientists, however, are not ready to believe in only one reality because they are unable to solve the puzzle—which came first, the hen or the egg? Therefore, for them, there are at least two primary realities—physical and metaphysical—which can be divided into a few more sub-realities. In this context, Thomas Kutscher's Multi-Layered Reality (MLR) Model is worth quoting because he says that the reality is multi-layered and the total number is eight. Starting from lowest to highest, he has given the following list of physical (1 to 4) and metaphysical (5 to 8) realities:

1. The layer of physical laws, matter and physical energy.
2. The layer of form, design, and basic inorganic processes and other non-biological physical reality.

3. The layer of organic and genetic biochemistry including basic microbiological design and processes that support life.
4. The morphogenesis layer of advanced design, form, structure, development, evolution, and mutations of all living things.
5. The layer that includes the spirit/soul and the metaphysical mind that survives death.
6. The karmic and metaphysical shaping layer that includes ***karma***, astrology and other systems that force the development, lessons and corrections needed for all people.
7. The soul guidance layer including non-physical entities that are spiritually and consciously evolved such that they have transcended reincarnation and ***karma***.
8. The layer of Universal Mind or God.

Dr. Gina Cerminera has also provided two different lists to throw sufficient light on metaphysical realities. These lists—one about the Essential Truths and the other about General Advice—are based on numerous readings provided by Edgar Cayce:

Essential Truths

- God exists.
- Every soul is a portion of God.
- Life is purposeful.
- Life is continuous.
- All human life operates under law (*Karma*, reincarnation, etc.).
- Love fulfils that law.
- The will of man/woman creates his/her destiny.
- The mind of man/woman has formative power.

- The answer to all problems is within the self.

General Advice

- Realize first your relationship to the Creative Forces of the Universe, or God.
- Formulate your ideals and purposes in life.
- Strive to achieve those ideals.
- Be active.
- Be patient.
- Be joyous.
- Leave the results to God.
- Do not seek to evade any problem.
- Be a channel of good to others.

It is thus clear that there are several dynamic layers of reality which can be grouped broadly under two major heads: physical and metaphysical. They are tightly integrated with each other like body, mind, and soul of a person, and they affect us all the time. They cannot be separated or counted exactly, but they can be understood through their functions. It will be in our interest to know about all these realities and maintain a balance among them. It has been rightly said by Edgar Cayce that "Spirit is the life, Mind is the builder, and Physical is the result." Through proper understanding of these three entities—Spirit, Mind, and Body—anyone can get the wisdom to solve various problems and remain happy for ever. Unfortunately, many of us, in the name of science, are trying to know only about physical realities. But such efforts will never give us complete picture unless we learn also to pay proper attention to metaphysical realities. Perhaps this is the reason why, in spite of thousand and thousand researches in every subject, we have not got the truth as yet.

Purpose of this Book

We know it well that the scientific psychology, developed by Watson and Freud, dominated throughout the history of psychology till 1960. Since this scientific psychology had no regard for the inner dimension of human life, humanistic psychology was started as a movement by Maslow and others to explore the hidden talents and higher reaches of the human mind. Out of this Humanistic movement, under the influence of Eastern traditions like Buddhism and Hinduism, another movement of transpersonal psychology also started. Both these movements became popular in parts of the U.S. and Europe and slowly began to spread in some other parts of the world. But, in spite of their popularity and serious attempts made by Ken Wilber to create a comprehensive system, they remained as a body of diverse developments without a unified underlying philosophical vision.

At this turning point, fortunately, with the dawn of the twenty first century, we have got a new psychological system known as *Integral Psychology* which promises to explore and understand the totality of the human phenomenon. It covers the entire body-mind-psyche-spirit spectrum and encompasses the previously explored unconscious and the conscious dimensions of the psyche, as well as the supraconscious dimension traditionally excluded from psychological inquiry. According to Bahman Shirazi, if defined properly, integral psychology is "the final wave of development in the current history of psychology." This integral psychology, as claimed by Indra Sen, is completely based on Sri Aurobindo's broader metaphysical outlook maintained in philosophy, psychology, and management.

Being inspired by this new system of integral psychology in general and Sri Aurobindo's metaphysical teachings in particular, this book has been compiled from various sources to deal with metaphysical realities in psychology and management. This is a collection of my selected articles published in national and international journals and are based on my life-long experience of teaching psychology and management courses to the undergraduate and postgraduate students. Being dissatisfied with the "scientific" psychology, for the last ten years, I have been writing on human mind, behaviour, intuitive awareness, love, spirituality, dream, *karma*, reincarnation, etc., and have been pleading for including Intuition as a method of psychology. Time has come now for each one of us to change our mindset and realize the importance of metaphysical realities in all walks of life.

In short, this book is about learning to listen to intuition, the voice of Spirit within us. This will help us in finding out our own sense of order and structure in our personal, professional and spiritual life.

M.B. Sharan
Ex-Professor of Psychology
and
Head Deptt. of Humanities & Social Science
IIT, Kharagpur

1

Making Psychology Complete and Essential for Understanding of the Human Mind, Behaviour and Intuitive Awareness

(Presidential Address delivered at 16th Annual Conference of the National Academy of Psychology held at IIT, Bombay from December 14 to 16, 2006)

I have taught psychology to under-graduate and post-graduate students of Patna University, Bhagalpur University, and IIT, Kharagpur for more than four decades. I have also taught some of the management courses to these students in IIT and in Vinod Gupta School of Management (VGSOM). This teaching of management I am still continuing in Rourkela Institute of Management Studies (RIMS), Rourkela even after my retirement from IIT service. I must say, I have always enjoyed maximum in a classroom while teaching these subjects. I have also been listening to my psychologist-colleagues and management experts in national and international conferences on different subjects. From all these, I can say with confidence that psychology has contributed a lot to me, to my colleagues in psychology and management, and to many others and, as a subject, it has been successful within its own defined area of study.

However, a few basic questions have been bothering me for quite some time. If psychology has become today the science of behaviour and mental processes, as defined by Myers (1995), do we understand fully what is behaviour? What is mind? What is mental process? Is it possible to know about all these subject matters through the objective or scientific methods we are using in psychology? Is psychology really understanding all the social problems and solving them? Is it really helping others and do people have respect for this subject? These are some of the questions we need to answer honestly. Is it not a fact that all questions related to mind and behaviour cannot be answered in psychology because, for the most part, it has adopted the scientific methods which allow psychologists to study only such questions which can be tested in a precise, objective, and publicly verifiable fashion? Have not we been trained to formulate hypotheses and collect data to test their validity either through controlled laboratory experiments or through questionnaires? Sometimes, we are allowed to gather information through some other methods like observations, interviews, clinical studies, and surveys. But what about such aspects of mind and behaviour like faith, trust, confidence, consciousness, spirituality, wisdom, *karma*, etc. which cannot be tested objectively? Should we simply drop them from the subject matters of psychology as Watson did to make psychology a natural science? Or, should we think of some other methods to study such subjects in psychology? It is good that psychology is gaining consciousness today by including mental processes in its definition. But it would be still better, if it also includes another suitable method to study such subject matters. This will give us a chance to understand all the aspects of human mind and behaviour and will encourage us to listen to others on these subjects who have made significant contributions in these areas. My life-long experience to this point says that this will also make psychology complete and essential for understanding of the human mind, behaviour, and intuitive awareness. Indian thinkers and psychologists (e.g., Mehta, 2000; Daftuar, 2002; Rao, 2002; Rao, 2005; Rao & Marwaha, 2005; Sharma, 2005; Sharan, 2005a, 2005b) have been talking about these subjects on different occasions and, I am sure, they can contribute a lot in this regard because many of them have got intuitive minds. We should not forget that modern psychology has the dual roots of philosophy and science and its scope has broadened considerably in recent years to include many such topics which Watson and other early behaviourists would not have tolerated.

Human Mind: Conscious, Subconscious or Unconscious?

The nature of human mind is difficult to understand because it is very subtle as well as hidden. Therefore, it has been defined in different ways by different authors or by the same author on different occasions. Freud originally presented a topographical model of mind and defined it in terms of conscious, preconscious and unconscious—'conscious' as the part of the psyche that includes material of which one is fully aware; 'preconscious' as the part of the psyche that includes material which is not at the moment within one's awareness but which can readily be brought to the conscious mind; and 'unconscious' as the part of the psyche that includes material not within one's awareness and which cannot readily be brought to the conscious mind (Ewen, 1980). But he put maximum emphasis on the unconscious mind. Today, however, a debate is going on between the "minds" and many are telling us to maintain a balance between these minds, as it is "one". Bandler and Grinder (1979) have rightly tried to settle the issue by saying that they are different in just a way of describing events—'conscious' as whatever we are aware of at a moment, and 'unconscious' as everything else—otherwise, as a whole, it is one. They are citing a very convincing example in their support: Suppose we are driving along the highway returning home; on approaching the neighbourhood, we start realizing that for the past several minutes our mind has been elsewhere. Daydreaming, thinking about things, our mind has been on anything but paying attention to the road. We wonder how we managed to watch out for cars, follow traffic signals, and make the right turns when we were "not there". Thus, there are a number of things we are doing without paying proper attention to all at a time and the pendulum of awareness swings between the "minds" without any difficulty.

Now, the next question is: By which name this one mind should be known? Those who are working in the field of information processing say that the conscious awareness is just the tip of the iceberg. It simply enables us to exert voluntary control and to communicate our mental states to others (Kihlstrom, 1987). Beneath the surface, actually, subconscious information processing occurs simultaneously on many parallel tracks. When we look at a flying bird, we are consciously aware of the result of our cognitive processes but not of our sub-processing of the bird's colour, form, movement, distance and identity. Therefore, from the functional viewpoint, it is the subconscious mind which takes care of all the processes that are occurring out of conscious awareness. This one mind thus should be known as the subconscious mind (Murphy, 2000).

Philosophers and some other thinkers, however, attach more importance to the conscious part of the mind. They say that it is the conscious part of the mind which does all the processing of information because it is logical, reasonable, and can change its point of view at will. Since the subconscious mind is not logical and reasonable, it cannot take any independent decision of its own, and it has to simply support the conscious mind. This idea of conscious mind has been fully supported by Vedanta (philosophy and religion based on the Vedas teach the non-duality of the individual soul and God). It throws sufficient light not only on what mind is, and why it should be known as the conscious mind, but also on how it is illuminated by the power of consciousness. According to Vedanta, the mind is known *as antahkarana* (internal instrument) which perceives through five sense organs—eyes, ears, nose, tongue, and skin—and acts through five organs of action—the organ of speech, the hands, the legs, the organ of procreation, and the organ of evacuation. Thus, it recognizes different functions of the mind and thereby assumes that all these functions are possible only through the conscious mind. The power of consciousness, however, Vedanta says further, is not the built-in-characteristic of the mind. This comes from some higher source known as *Soul, Atman* or *Self.* Since mind is not the real perceiver or knower of the mental phenomenon, Vedanta differentiates between the mind and the Self—the mind as an object (the known) and the Self as a subject (the knower). Anything that falls into the category of the known does not have consciousness as its very essence whereas the subject or knower does. Thus, there is one ultimate observer or experiencer, and that is the Self. This is the reason why today many are of the opinion that there are three distinct factors of human personality—the physical body, the mind, and the soul. They are vitally connected and though they appear to be one single entity, they are distinguishable. Thus, it can be safely concluded that one should not get caught by the words 'conscious', 'subconscious' and 'unconscious' because they are just to describe different functions of the same mind. Each of these is accessible to us in some way because they communicate with each other in their own way. This one mind, therefore, should be best known as the conscious mind.

From Conscious Mind to Superconscious Mind

We have seen what wonderful arrangements we have within us of mind and soul. Mind, which is like an instrument, is getting the power of consciousness from soul. That means our mind is functioning like a mirror which can perceive properly only when it is fully illuminated by our soul. Since soul, like sun, is throwing light constantly on the mirror, it is for the mind to absorb them properly. If it is neat and clean, it will absorb better; otherwise, it will not be able to do so. In this sense, Vedanta rightly says that it is possible for us to make our conscious mind "Superconscious" which will perceive and judge things in a better way making use of all the informations available in the so called subconscious and unconscious minds. Thus, for the development of the Superconscious Mind, we need to feed the conscious mind with rich food, nourish it regularly, strengthen it, and enrich it. According to Vedanta, "The richest soil, the soil of the human mind, lies fallow. If it could be tilled well it would yield golden crops, but since it lies fallow, it yields brambles and thorny bushes and weeds" (Ellis, 1994).

From perception viewpoint, Sharma (2005) has also identified three quantum states of mind: the state of Ordinary

Perception (OP), the state of Extra-Sensory Perception (ESP), and the state of Extraordinary Perception (EOP). Many of us are working with the first state of mind, and therefore, most of the times we are having ordinary perceptions including illusions and hallucinations. But there are occasions we also work with the second state of mind and experience some kind of extrasensory perceptions like telepathy and precognition. At the same time, there are some persons who sometimes work with the third state of mind and have extraordinary perceptions. Scientists and creative persons perhaps get something new only in this state of intuitive mind. Superconscious Mind thus refers to this state of mind when we experience cosmic connectivity and have good understanding, peace, wisdom and enlightenment.

The Universal Mind

The Superconscious Mind is also known as the "Universal Mind." Many years ago, Jung proposed a psychoanalytic theory based on what he called archetypes of a universal unconscious. "These archetypes are a set of universal patterns from which all symbols evolve. They point to a region of the mind that exists as a common link between all people, living and dead." Since Freud did not agree with Jung's collective unconscious, the transpersonal mind remained neglected all these years. Recently, however, many have started attaching importance to this transpersonal mind because it has many spiritual and moral possibilities hidden within it. According to Ellis (1994), "It holds possibilities which are locked away from the conscious mind, for it has at its disposal all subliminal psychic contents, all those things which have been forgotten or overlooked, as well as the wisdom and experience of uncounted centuries which are laid down in its archetypal organs....The unconscious can serve man as a unique guide, provided he can resist the lure of being misguided. Superconscious Mind is thus the soul's mind which is connected to all others' minds. Edgar Cayce has given a pictorial model of the link between minds (Reed, 1989). It shows there is one mind and people share it (see Figures 1.1 and 1.2).

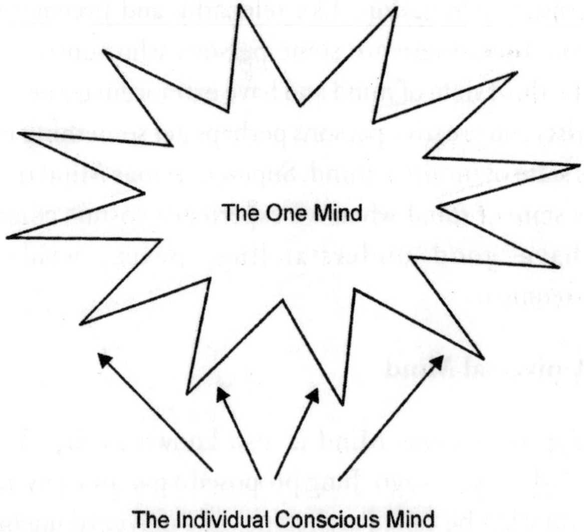

Fig. 1.1: The Relations between Individual Conscious Minds and the One Mind

In Figure 1.1, which is a multipoint star, Cayce shows how the star itself represents the entire mind. Each arm of the star represents a portion of the mind for a different person. The very tip of each point represents the conscious mind of an individual.

In Figure 1.2, we see how the unconscious mind is a continuous connective layer of the inner parts of the mind's arms. The star tips only seem separate from one another. The arms of the stars are clearly like fingers on the same hand. The arms represent our subconscious minds. All subconscious minds are connected. The core of the mind is available to us all *via* the Superconscious Mind. The relationship among the

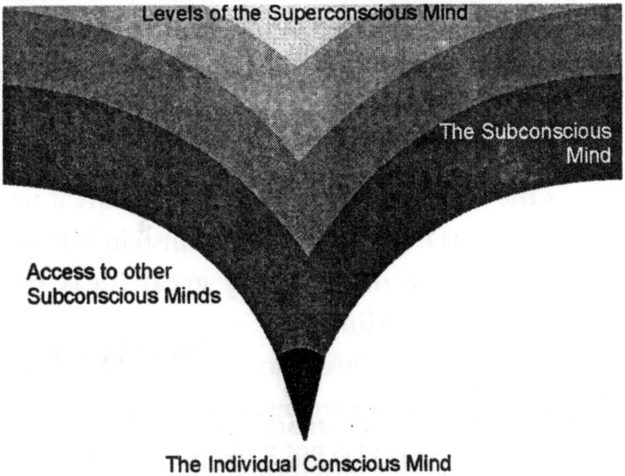

Fig. 1.2: Regions of the Mind

Conscious, Subconscious, and Superconscious Mind is thus something like this (see Figure 1.3) as suggested by Koh (2004):

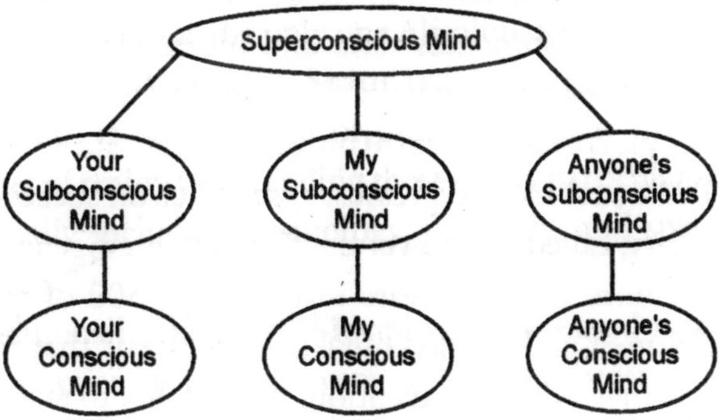

Fig. 1.3: Connection between Minds

From the diagram, we can see that we are all connected at the superconscious level, through our individual's subconscious mind. The conscious mind is not connected directly to the Superconscious Mind. Koh maintains that:

- There is only one Superconscious Mind (the Universal Mind), to which all of our minds are connected. It is like a mega computer that orchestrates the activities in every little computer connected to it.
- It helps us to make good decisions, since it has infinite intelligence. It has all the answers we want, including tomorrow's share price!
- It is the source of all true inventions. Great inventors like Thomas Edison and Albert Einstein have mastered the technique of receiving great ideas from the Superconscious Mind.
- It helps us to achieve our goals. Once we truly understand the Superconscious Mind Power, we will realize that success is not a function of luck.

Tapping the Superconscious Mind

We have seen that our Superconscious Mind can access every piece of information stored in our conscious and subconscious minds. It can also access data and ideas outside our own experience, because it actually lies outside our human mind. That is why it is called a form of universal or infinite intelligence. Hill (2004), perhaps the greatest researcher on success of the 20th century, called this power the "infinite intelligence." After spending more than 20 years interviewing 500 of the most successful men and women alive in America at that time, he concluded that, without exception, their ability to tap into this higher form of infinite intelligence was the primary reason for their great success in life. We, therefore, need to learn about how to tap this Superconscious Mind which is the source of all examples of pure creativity. According to Tracy (2002), the critical factor in using our Superconscious Mind is our attitude.

Our Superconscious Mind functions best with an attitude of calm, confident expectations. When we adopt an attitude of faith and acceptance, when we confidently accept and believe that everything that is happening to us is moving us progressively towards the achievement of our goal, our Superconscious Mind seems to come alive, like all the lights have been turned on in a room. That is why successful people seem to have tremendous clarity concerning what they want, along with tremendous calmness and confidence regarding their ability to achieve it. This combination of attitudes will throw the power switch on our superconscious abilities. Because of such superconscious powers, anything that we can hold in our mind on a continuing basis, we can have. We believe in the divine statement that "As you sow, so you reap"; and this law of consequences refers to mental states; to our thoughts. Based on this assumption, Tracy (2002), one of the world's leading authorities on personal and business success, has given a 10-step plan for plugging into our superconscious power to get what we truly want in life. He asserts that "make this plan a regular habit and you will be astonished at the results." By doing so, you will move from the "positive thinking" of the hopeful person to the "positive knowing" of the totally successful person.

- Decide exactly what you want.
- Write your goal clearly in every detail.
- Write your goal in simple, present tense words on a three-by-five index card and carry it with you to read and re-read throughout the day whenever you get a chance.
- Make a list of everything you can think of that you can do that will move you towards your goal.
- Organize the list by priority—what is more important and what is less important?

- Resolve to take action everyday on one of the items on your list.
- Visualize your goal repeatedly.
- Get the feeling of pleasure and enjoyment that you would have if your goal was realized at this moment.
- Confidently behave as if your Superconscious Mind were bringing your goal into reality.
- Release your goal completely to your Superconscious Mind.

Similar views have been expressed by many other Western thinkers like Stone (2006), Murphy (2000), Reed and English (2002), etc. Indian thinkers, however, differ in their approach. They teach about how to purify body and how to purify mind to control the mind. And, for them (Budhananda, 2005; Vivekananda, 2005), the entire secret of controlling the mind is: *abhyasa* (practice) and *vairagya* (dispassion). "...Practice and Dispassion must co-exist if one is to come to a perfect control of the mind.... Practice is possible only by being a participant in the daily activities aimed at sustenance or betterment, whether individual or collective. But Dispassion suggests a stepping out of activities; it indicates a condition of being a witness to what is happening" (Mehta, 2000).

Human Behaviour: Physical, Mental or Spiritual?

We have seen how American psychologists defined psychology as "the science of observable behaviour" and, therefore, many of the studies in psychology remained restricted to only overt activities for many, many years. But, today, we are not agreeing with the behaviourists and are studying many subjective aspects as well. Not only that, we also try to explain every human behaviour in terms of 'mind' involved in it. We assume that every human behaviour is having minimum two aspects—the *physical* and the *mental*—the physical related to body and the mental, related to mind. Since we want to maintain a balance between mind and body in order to have an "effective" behaviour, the behaviour becomes "*spiritual*" in nature due to Gestalt effect. This can be explained through the example of understanding love in a laboratory. Is it not a fact that by putting love under scientific scrutiny, researchers have misunderstood it by destroying its mystery? In reality, love includes affection and anger, excitement and boredom, stability and change, bond and freedom, etc. All these cannot be understood by any scientific method. As a result, those researchers, who have tried to know about it by using all sorts of sophisticated instruments, have found it to be a triangle of which the three sides represent physiological, psychological, and anthropological factors. But, outside the laboratory, the "true love" has emerged as a circle which combines all the three kinds of factors into one. This combination in equal proportion, as a whole, is known as "spiritual love". This is such a nice blend that no factor is trying to dominate upon the other one. This kind of "spiritual love" cannot be analyzed in a laboratory but can be experienced. Like this, every human behaviour needs to be effective (*spiritual*) and needs to be understood finally by experience. And such experience is known as "*Intuitive Experience*".

Human Action: Behaviour or *Karma*?

For many Western researchers, human action is just a behaviour. But for Indian thinkers, it is more than that—"*karma*"—which refers to one's intention or motivation while doing an action. According to Tsering (2004), intention is the most important of all mental events because it gives direction to the mind, determining whether we engage with virtuous, non-virtuous, or neutral objects. Just as iron is powerlessly drawn to a magnet, our minds are powerlessly drawn to the object of our intentions. Intention may be expressed through either physical or verbal actions. Actually, Indian thinkers differentiate between human and animal behaviours. They argue that in the case of animals, instinct prevails, but in the case of human beings, reason prevails. Therefore, only human beings—not animals—have the freedom and capacity to judge rightly or wrongly about their behaviours. This exercise of judgement is known as *karma* and this makes human life as the *karma-bhumi*:

> *"Watch your thoughts, for they become words.*
> *Watch your words, for they become actions.*
> *Watch your actions, for they become habits.*
> *Watch your habits, for they become character.*
> *Watch your character, for it becomes your destiny."*
>
> —Unknown source

How *Karma* Works

Karma is a Sanskrit word which literally means '*action*'. But it also signifies cause and effect relationship. We believe in the divine statement: "As you sow, so shall you reap" like the third law of Newton: 'Each action has an equal and opposite reaction.' We also believe that the soul travels from one body to the next and the force that drives the process of rebirth of the soul is an element of *karma*. Thus, for Hindus and Buddhists, *karma* is the mental and physical deeds that determine the effects of our life and rebirth and can be consequences from our previous lives or from actions in this one. Recently, some Western thinkers like Edgar Cayce, McArthur and Carmen Harra have also started believing in the same way: "Human beings come into a body alone and when we shed our body we die alone. The only thing we take with us are our memories, our *karma*" (Harra, 2002).

This shows clearly that all of us are governed by the universal "karmic law" and there is nothing by chance. Whether we realize it or not, everyday we are creating *karma* with every thought and action. Either we kill an insect, abuse someone, or are jealous of a friend, we are creating bad *karma*. Similarly, every single thing we do each day that is positive like helping a person, aiding a beggar, or showing sympathy and love creates good *karma*. In this sense, life is a constant balancing act of offsetting the bad *karmas* with the good ones. If we don't erase our bad *karmas* or heal them at the end of everyday, they will accumulate. Such accumulated *karmas*—accumulated over time and sometimes over many lifetimes—work like the "snowball effect". They go on multiplying and multiplying. We, therefore, need to resolve negative *karmas* everyday by regular prayer (confession) and by more and more positive acts. Otherwise, they will never be healed, and we have to live with the consequential sufferings.

Our largest obstacle to understanding or even believing in *karma* may be time. The 're-actions' or results of our actions show up with a time delay, and it becomes extremely hard to tell which action caused which result. Actions done in a previous life can create results in this life, but who can remember their past lives? For ordinary humans, the mechanisms of *karma* can be intellectually understood to some extent, but never completely "seen". However, every mainstream religion teaches us about the consequences of our actions. The explanations may differ, but does it really matter in the end whether the law of *karma* causes us trouble or God Himself in His final judgement?

How do we accumulate karmic seeds? Every physical and verbal action is preceded by mental activity. Goodwill motivates a kind gesture; ill will motivates nasty words. Ill will is the intention to cause mental, emotional or physical harm. Thus, before and during a bad action, ill will is present in our mind. The presence of ill will before and during this act has an impact on the mind due to which a certain potential is left behind. This potential is a karmic seed, a seed planted in our mind by physical, verbal or mental action. The strength or depth of this seed is determined by a number of factors, including how strong our intention is, whether we clearly understand what we are doing, whether we act on our intention, and whether the physical and verbal action is completed. Seeds will remain in the mind until they ripen or are destroyed. Seeds left by negative mental events and actions can be destroyed by some opponent or antidotal powers. The most important of these powers are regrets for the negative acts and a firm resolve not to act that way again in the future.

Karmic Resolution

Every thought and action creates memory and comes back either to bless or haunt us. This is what makes us unique and composes our lives. It also creates a field of information around us at the level of energy. We store this information in our field like data in a computer. This data or memory is either positive or negative. All the negative memory will resurface in our life again and again, and the only way to move forward is to resolve it. Reincarnation is thus one opportunity to repair what we did wrong. It is an opportunity to come back and repent, to ask for forgiveness and change what we did wrong. Life is thus a process of introspecting our thoughts and actions and resolving the bad *karmas* everyday. This can be achieved through purifying the mind and following the Karmic Resolution Method as suggested by Harra (2002):

1. *Deep Breathing*: Breath not only gives life, it also creates a bridge between the subconscious and conscious mind and connects the mind and body.
2. *Memory Meditation*: It is a powerful tool for allowing our conscious mind to access what is at work in our subconscious mind.
3. *Expanding Emotional Awareness*: Sometimes we react in a heightened way because of karmic memory or connection that is hidden in our unconscious mind. Expanding awareness allows us to break the cycle of inappropriate emotions.
4. *Recognizing and Breaking Negative Patterns*: When we understand which emotions are dominating our life and begin to view them objectively, we may recognize some negative recurring patterns. Such patterns or grip which they have on our life must be broken.
5. *Restoring Equilibrium:* We should use our conscious mind as reprogramming of the subconscious mind by using imagery that replaces all negative thoughts and beliefs with positive ones.
6. *Designing a Vision for the Future*: After breaking all negative thoughts and emotions and replacing them by positive ones, we can begin to visualize a new way of living.
7. *Gathering Powerful Positive Energy:* In order to create a new reality we would need to recharge our batteries by tapping into the energy of the Invisible World.
8. *Affirmations for the New Reality:* We need personal affirmations, which should come from deep within, to reinforce our vision and keep the energy of the Universe focused.
9. *Prayers for Gratitude and Happiness*: The most important way of celebrating our new life is through

acknowledging the universal life force and kindness of God.

10. *Recording and Tracking the Progress in a Journal:* Writing things regularly help to clarify our thoughts and record our progress on different karmic issues.

We should always remember that the Universe wants us to be happy and fulfilled and to travel on the path of spirituality. There are many persons who have achieved karmic success on this path only through regular prayer and meditation.

Intuitive Awareness: The Key to Understanding and Healthy Living

The term "intuition" means exactly what it sounds like—intuition—an inner tutor or teaching and learning mechanism that takes us forward daily. The dictionary defines intuition as "the perception of truths, facts, etc. without reasoning; the immediate knowledge or learning of something without the conscious use of reasoning; instantaneous apprehension" (Denning, 2001). Swami Omkarananda (1999) also says "Intuition is the immediate knowledge of the Absolute, obtained through the eye of wisdom, as opposed to the knowledge of the external objects derived through the exercise of the senses and the intellect. It is truth obtained by internal apprehension, without the aid of perception or the operation of the reasoning powers. It is a direct vision and apprehension of the Divine Reality underlying the manifested and the unmanifested Universe." That means, it is a process which perceives things without relying on the senses and gives us a kind of creative awareness by interpreting all the information in a holistic way (Sharan, 2005b). Seale (2002) has rightly said, "Intuition is spiritual energy, not psychic energy. Psychic energy is purely mental energy, and limited to mental energy, while spiritual energy embraces the totality of the Universe. Spiritual energy acknowledges that there is profound knowledge and wisdom available when we become one with Spirit or the universal consciousness." Intuition is thus both a vehicle for profound spiritual knowledge and for success and enjoyment in our daily lives.

Seale (2002) maintains further that intuitive awareness is a gift of talent which everyone has to some degree and which can be developed to guide and direct our lives in powerful and transformative ways. Just as we develop other gifts and talents for use in daily lives, it is our responsibility to fully develop our own intuitive gifts in order to be true partners with Spirit in the co-creation of our lives. Even Einstein, one of the towering intellects of modern time, remarked once that "The intuitive mind is a sacred gift and the rational mind is a faithful servant. We have created a society that honours the servant and has forgotten the gift."

Intuitive awareness thus simply means living life superconsciously. When we live our lives mindlessly or with ordinary mind, we begin to take on the attributes of whatever is around us, both positive and negative, being easily swayed by the forces and opinions of others. But when we live mindfully—with full attention given to each and every moment in our life—we begin to glow in our own light and truth. We come to know who we are, what our life purpose is, what our real motivation is, and what gives us passion. We begin to step into our own power and strength, and develop as individuals with unique gifts and talents (Sumedho, 2004).

In the Buddhist tradition, there is actually a practice called mindfulness. Mindfulness is simply focusing our attention on wherever we are and whatever we are doing at each moment. It is a state of becoming fully awaken to who we are, what we think and feel, what the present moment is about, and clearly seeing our views of the world. It is thus a heightened state of awareness, opening us to the full spectrum of possibilities. "This practice of mindfulness or conscious living is an important step towards focusing our lives and developing intuitive awareness. The more we can focus our full attention on where we are and what we are doing in any given moment, the more we become fully aware of all that is there for us" (Seale, 2002).

Many belief systems teach that staying present or being 'mindful' is the basic principle behind inner peace and contentment which leads to intuitive awareness. Being mindful means giving full concentration to whatever we are doing in the present, having no real awareness of anything else, becoming completely absorbed, lost in the activity and the moment. According to Clare (2003), "this experience of the moment means we are more likely to notice things around us...." This suggests that intuitive awareness comes to a person only when he or she has the intuitive state of mind. It involves more than simply "going with our gut" or "trusting our hunches". It is also not synchronicity. It prompts a person to think in certain ways that create the results which contribute to well-being, allowing synchronicity to manifest (Denning, 2001). Reed and English (2002) also maintain that by paying attention to the thoughts, feelings, and images that come to mind, we are learning to tune into our intuition which is a natural gift born in everyone. But it becomes most effective in a person who learns to develop "The Intuitive Heart" by caring and loving his/her own inner self and of others. In order to have the intuitive awareness through the intuitive heart, they suggest the following six steps:

1. *Learn from Your Breath to Trust Your Intuitive Inspiration:* Focus on your breathing and discover how you can trust it to flow naturally, spontaneously, with no effort or control on your part. Intuitive inspiration will come to you automatically.
2. *Make the Heart Connection:* Let gratitude fill your heart, allowing you to release all concerns. Your heart energy naturally begins to expand. Focus it on the target of your search for intuition.
3. *Invite a Memory:* Ask for one of your millions of personal memories to pop into your mind. Without intentionally choosing it, but accepting the first one that comes, trust that within your heart is stored the perfect memory that is right for this occasion.
4. *Tell Your Story*: Explore the experience that surrounds that memory. Let your memory be the seed of a story—here's what was going on, here's what happened, here's how it turned out.
5. *Search Your Heart for Wisdom*: See what lessons your story holds. What truth does it contain? What did you learn from that experience? What does this story teach you today?
6. *Learn from Feedback:* Note how the teaching story relates to the focus of your quest for intuition. How can you use this new perspective to respond to your current situation differently?

Conclusion

We cannot deny the fact that psychology developed out of philosophical speculations as to the nature of man when these came to be influenced by the advances in the biological sciences.

From this union, psychology retained a philosophical, speculative character and a dualistic mind/body approach to behaviour and 'mental life'. Watson tried to make it a division of natural science by dropping *experience* from its definition and his 'behaviourism' emerged as the methodology which dominated academic psychology for the next half-century. But, in spite of its extensive and remarkably enduring influence, it warranted criticism. Today, with general acceptance, it has been defined again as the scientific study of both human behaviour and human experience. This has definitely broadened the scope of psychology and has made us realize that the *science* of psychology cannot exclude *experience* from its study.

However, it is also a fact that if psychology has now come of age, it is because it has achieved a more adequate 'form of knowledge' (Gillham, 1976). Today, psychologists construct theories that organize observations and imply testable hypotheses. To describe, predict, and explain behaviour and mental processes, they use several methods like Introspection, Naturalistic Observation, Questionnaire and Survey, Case Study, Correlation, and Experimentation. Not only that, they are also trying seriously to capture consciousness or spirituality in their studies. Whether described as "inner journey" or "enlightenment" or "wisdom", it is a domain attracting unprecedented interest and psychologists are rushing to fill the void. According to Hoffman (2002), "In coming years, we'll surely see scientific validation on the connection between our spiritual well-being at work and our highest productivity, involving both mind and body. Undoubtedly, the task of assessing intrinsic spirituality will play an increasingly vital role in that domain."

Now, the question is: How to study spirituality or consciousness in psychology? With the available methods listed above, it may perhaps be difficult to understand the issue and discern the truth. Every method has been found to be suffering from certain limitations. Even the experimental method, which is considered to be the ultimate method of psychology today, is subject to certain serious constraints. "For many thoughtful students the idea of applying science to human affairs raises concerns about how well experiments relate to life, how experimenters treat human and animal subjects, and how psychologists' values influence their work and its applications" (Myers, 1995). In such situation, as suggested by many Indian thinkers like Radhakrishnan (McDermott, 1970), Omkarananda (1999), and now being supported by a good number of Western researchers (e.g., Coleman, 2000; Denning, 2001; Fitz, 2001; Seale, 2002; Clare, 2003; Peirce, 2005), psychologists need to realize the importance of Intuition as a method of psychology. This will help not only in understanding of the Superconscious Mind and effective (spiritual) behaviour of the human beings but also in getting the truth obtained through other methods. It has been rightly said that without following intuition, intellectuals will remain imperfect and divided, and blind to the truth behind the appearances. "Intuition is the only way by which the Absolute can be realized and experienced in all its totality. The mortal, finite, limited senses and the intellect cannot comprehend the Reality which is immortal and all-pervading" (Omkarananda, 1999). This is the reason why all *Courses in Miracles* are teaching today to have regular prayer (how to talk to God) and meditation (how to listen to God) to have His Grace for developing *Intuitive Mind.* We all have this system in place but, the irony is, we have not yet learned how to use it fully.

References

Bandler, R. and Grinder, J. (1979). *Frogs into princes: Neuro-linguistic programming*. UT: Real People Press.

Budhananda, Swami. (2005). *The mind and its control* (25th Reprint). Kolkata: Advaita Ashrama.

Clare, S. (2003). *Trust your intuition.* (2nd Ed.). Delhi: Macmillan India.

Coleman, J.E. (2000). *The quiet mind.* New Delhi: New Age Books.

Daftuar, C.N. (2002). Spirit, mind and body connection: A new field for research in psychology. Paper presented at National Conference on "Yoga and Indian Approaches to Psychology" at Pondicherry from September 29 to October 1.

Day, L. (1996). *Practical intuition.* New York: Broadway books.

Denning, H.M. (2001). *Intuition and synchronicity.* Virginia: A.R.E. Press.

Ellis, R. (Ed.). (1994). *Mind: According to Vedanta.* Madras: Sri Ramakrishna Math.

Ewen, R.B. (1980). *An introduction to theories of personality.* New York: Academic Press.

Fitz, H.K. (2001). *Intuition: Its nature and uses in human experience.* Delhi: Motilal Banarsidass.

Gillham, W.E.C. (1976). *Psychology today.* London: Hodder and Stoughton.

Harra, C. (2002). *Everyday karma.* New York: Ballantine Books.

Hill, N. (2004). *Law of success.* The 21st century edition. New York: High Roads Media.

Hoffman, E. (2002). *Psychological testing at work.* New York: McGraw-Hill.

Kihlstrom, J.F. (1987). The cognitive unconscious. *Science*, 237, 1445-1452.

Koh, K. (2004). Mind power explained. www.subconscioussecrets.com

McArthur, B. (1993). *Your life: Why it is the way it is and what you can do about it.* Virginia: A.R.E. Press.

McDermott, R.A. (Ed.). (1970). *Basic writings of S. Radhakrishnan.* Bombay: Jaico Publishing House.

Mehta, R. (2000). *From mind to super-mind.* Delhi: Motilal Banarsidass.

Murphy, J. (2000). *The power of your subconscious mind.* New York: Bantam Books.

Myers, D.G. (1995). *Psychology* (4th Ed.). New York: Worth Publishers.

Omkarananda, Swami. (1999). The intuitive experience of the truth. www.omkarananda-ashram.net/intuitive.html

Peirce, P. (2005). *The intuitive way: The definitive guide to increasing your awareness.* OK: Council Oak Books.

Rao, K.R. (2002). *Consciousness studies: Cross-cultural perspectives.* Jefferson: McFarland & Co.

Rao, K.R. (2005). Psychology in the Indian tradition: A classical model with contemporary relevance. *Psychological Studies*, 50, 1-8.

Rao, Mrinalini. (2004). If you don't mind, it doesn't matter: A Vedantic exploration of mind as the object of the self. Paper presented at National Conference on "Indian Psychology, Yoga and Consciousness" at Pondicherry from December 10 to 13.

Rao, K.R. and Marwaha, S.B. (2005). *Towards a spiritual psychology: Essays in Indian psychology.* Delhi: Samvad India Foundation.

Reed, H. (1989). *Edgar Cayce on mysteries of the mind.* New York: Warner Books.

Reed, H. and English, B. (2002). *The intuitive heart.* Virginia: A.R.E. Press.

Seale, A. (2002). *Intuitive living.* New Delhi: New Age Books.

Sharan, M.B. (2005a). Vedantic approach to the understanding of human mind, behaviour and karma. *Indian Journal of Community Psychology*, 1, 1-9.

Sharan, M.B. (2005b). Understanding of human mind and behaviour: The missing link of intuitive experience. *Psychological Studies*, 50, 259-262.

Sharma, S. (2005). Quantum states of mind: Ordinary perception to extra-ordinary perception. *Psychological Studies*, 50, 9-15.

Stone, J.D. (2006). Integrated consciousness and how to develop the other 90 per cent of your mind. www.iamuniversity.com

Sumedho, A. (2004). *Intuitive awareness.* England: Amravati Publications.

Tracy, B. (2002). Tapping your superconscious mind. www.honorheart.com

Tsering, G.T. (2004). *The Buddha's medicine for the mind: Cultivating wisdom and compassion.* South Mellbourne, Vic.: Lothian Books.

Vivekananda, Swami. (2005). *Powers of the mind* (24th Impression). Kolkata: Advaita Ashrama.

2

Successful Intelligence, Creativity and Wisdom

What is Intelligence?

Till today, nobody knows exactly what intelligence is, although many attempts have been made to define it. For some, it is the ability to think abstractly; for some, it is reasoning; for some, it is solving mathematical problems; for some, it is to learn from experience; and so on. Thus, every person has his/her own definition, and even the psychologists differ on this question. Credit goes to a British psychologist, Spearman for offering one of the first influential theories of intelligence and defining it as an innate general ability. He found that when different tests of intelligence were intercorrelated, the correlations were usually positive. This suggested that different tests and test items were measuring some common factor. This he called general intelligence or 'g' factor (Spearman, 1927). Burt, who was greatly influenced by Spearman, and more recently, Eysenck and Jensen, have all supported the view that there is a common trait of intelligence which runs across much of a person's behaviour. They also call this to be a general factor or 'g' (Das, 1998).

Spearman maintained for many years that this general ability was one-dimensional in nature and was the basic mental energy. He said that intelligence was something like power which could not be seen with naked eyes but could be felt through its various functions. But when he found that an individual did not perform equally well on different types of cognitive tasks like mathematical, verbal, and so on, he thought that each type of task required a specific intellectual ability as well. He called these specific abilities 's' or specific factors. Thus for Spearman, finally, intelligence consisted of two factors—'g' and 's'.

Another psychologist, Thurstone (1938), however, did not agree with Spearman's general intelligence. He suggested that the intellect consisted of specific abilities. He called these components primary mental abilities and thus divided Spearman's general factor into seven factors: Number Ability (N), Word Fluency (W), Verbal Meaning (V), Memory (M), Reasoning (R), Spatial Relations (S), and Perceptual Speed (P). Thus for Thurstone, the general intelligence of Spearman represented a family of seven primary mental abilities.

It is a fact that two persons having the same IQ (intelligence quotient) differ in their intellectual abilities. Therefore, many intelligence tests are now being designed today to measure primary abilities instead of a heterogeneous agglomeration of such abilities. This, however, does not minimize the importance of "general intelligence" expressed in terms of IQ which is derived by dividing mental age (MA) by chronological age (CA), multiplied by 100. Thus, an average or "normal" IQ would be in the neighbourhood of 100—inferior ones below this value, and superior ones above it. Since IQs are distributed in accordance with the normal bell-shaped "probability" curve, it is possible to interpret them in accordance with the expectations that an IQ of a given magnitude will be encountered. About half (46.5%) of the IQs in any unselected population will fall between 90 and 109 and roughly the middle 65 per cent will be between 85 and 115. Only 1 to 2 per cent will be above 140 (genius), whereas 2 to 3 per cent will be below 70 (feebleminded). This kind of distribution of intelligence, by and large, has been maintained everywhere. Therefore, many are of the opinion that all is due to heredity and everyone is born with his/her own level of intelligence which cannot be changed.

Not all views of intelligence divide sharply on the unified/multifaceted issue. However, one influential perspective, proposed by Cattell (1963, 1987), adopts a more integral approach. According to Cattell, intelligence consists of two major components: fluid intelligence and crystallized intelligence. Fluid intelligence involves the abilities to form concepts, reasons and identify similarities. It is, therefore, more intuitive and is active in forming new mental structures rather than in making use of existing ones. In contrast, crystallized intelligence includes those aspects of intelligence which involve drawing on previously learned information to make decisions or solve problems. Classroom tests, vocabulary tests, and many social situations involve crystallized intelligence.

Now the question is: where does the pendulum of scientific opinion rest today? According to Baron (1995), it is somewhere in the middle. "Today most psychologists believe that intelligence involves both a general ability to handle a wide range of cognitive tasks and problems and a number of more specific abilities." In fact, modern thinking about the nature of intelligence has largely moved beyond the unitary-*versus*-multifaceted issue and is concentrating on how intelligence can be used for success in life.

Sternberg (2003) has rightly said that "...any serious understanding of intelligence must go beyond the standard paper and pencil tests currently in use. In addition to analytical and quantitative abilities, a theory of intelligence must take into account people's creative abilities—their ability to go beyond given information and imagine new and exciting ways of reforming old problems. It must also take into account, wisdom—people's ability to weigh options carefully and to act prudently."

Successful Intelligence

Successful intelligence can be defined as the ability to achieve success in life according to one's own definition of success within the socio-cultural context. Every individual has to deal with the kind of socio-psychological world in which he/she lives. He/she faces a particular environment of others who will make demands upon him/her, describe his/her behaviour in given ways, react to him/her with approval and disapproval, and act so as to facilitate or hinder with him/her various gains and losses. Confronted with such a complex system of requirements, facilities, and conditions of work, he/she effects his/her modes of adaptation and, in order to justify himself/herself, he/she gives his/her own definition. Some people choose to concentrate on extracurricular activities whereas others choose to do well in the academic activities. Some even prefer to do such things which are particularly meaningful to them and never try to change even if they are more rewarding financially. Thus, the definition of success for an individual is idiographic. The conceptualization of intelligence, however, is within the socio-cultural context. Being a religious person may be highly rewarded in one society and viewed as a worthless pursuit in another. According to Stenberg (2003), one's ability to achieve success depends on:

1. Capitalizing on strengths and correcting or compensating for weaknesses,
2. Adapting to new environment or modifying the environment to suit him or her,
3. Balancing the analytical, creative, and practical abilities.

At the end, however, Sternberg finds it difficult to draw anyone additive combination rule of emphasizing analytical, creative, and practical abilities. Based on his experience, he says that "there seems to be an infinite number of combination rules." This says indirectly that success is decided not only by these intellectual abilities but by something else (may be some divine power).

Creativity

Creativity is the ability to produce work that is novel (original or unexpected), high in quality, and appropriate (that is, useful). It is the cognitive activity which results in new or novel ways of viewing or solving problems. Most people would agree that creativity is desirable because it is from creativity that major inventions, scientific breakthroughs, and great works of music, literature, and art derive. Innovation, on the other hand, usually means the use of these ideas. In an organization, this can mean a new product, a new service, or a new way of doing things. It is implied that organizations not only generate new ideas but also translate them into practical applications.

While it is tempting to assume that creativity springs suddenly from flashes of inspiration or other heroic success, psychologists who have studied it concludes that the creative process consists of several specific activities that occur in series (Baron, 1995):

- First, creativity involves considerable preparation—gathering knowledge relevant to it, and working on it seriously. Edison rightly remarked once that "Success is ninety-eight percent perspiration and only two percent inspiration."
- Second, creative solutions often emerge after a period of incubation. In this stage, processing of information goes on in the conscious, subconscious and unconscious mind. Many times, persons feel frustrated and exhausted in this stage.
- Third, creativity does often involve a sudden illumination, or insight. At such times, individuals report that they suddenly get the solution to a problem they have been seeking for days and months.
- Fourth, the idea got through illumination is worked out, translated into testable form, and verified. Only when sufficient evidence indicates that it does work, creative solution is carried to a final decision.

Recently, getting the core idea of intuition from Dr. S. Radhakrishnan, a Western philosopher, Dr. Hope K. Fitz has presented her view that creativity like intuition is a natural or necessary part of the "mind's life" which needs to be developed. She argues that intuition is not a non-discursive form or independent way of gaining knowledge. It is simply one means to knowledge, which is complementary to reason, and can be verified by reason. Secondly, she introduces two kinds of intuition: 'penetrating insight' and 'creative insight' (Fitz, 2001). For her, penetrating insight is an insight into the structure of a problem, an insight into the threshold of "Revealed Being". Creative insight, on the other hand, has two forms: one form is an insight into a chain of links or transitions which can lead to the solution of a problem; another form is an insight into a series of events which may lead to an eventuality. This kind of insight is generally associated with acts of creativity (as used in art, architecture, poetry, etc.). And, finally, she pleads that "one must develop one's intuitive powers, just as one must develop one's intellectual powers."

Steps to Enhance Creativity

Thus, it is clear that creativity can be taught. Creative thoughts are often the fruits of extensive efforts and several techniques are available to nurture those kinds of thoughts. Sternberg (2003) has suggested twenty-one ways to develop creativity. However, from a practical viewpoint, some researchers (Isen the Baron, 1991; Schank, 1988) have suggested the following five steps to foster creativity:

1. *Develop a broad and rich knowledge base:* Creative solutions stem from the integration and combination of knowledge that is at the disposal of the person who wants to solve problems. Therefore, there seems to be no substitute for the hard work.
2. *Foster independence*: Creative people are willing to take risk and strike out on their own. If we wish to encourage creativity, we need to tolerate such independence and perhaps even seek to encourage its development.
3. *Encourage the use of analogies:* Many creative breakthroughs seem to involve the use of analogies—recognition of similarities between a new problem and an old one that has worked before.
4. *Encourage curiosity:* Creative people often have a high level of curiosity. They are interested in many different topics, they read widely, and they actively seek new experiences.

5. *Enhance positive effect:* Several studies concerned with the influence of effect or mood on cognition indicate that when people are in positive mood, they are often more creative than when they are in a neutral or negative mood.

Many belief systems teach that being 'mindful' is the basic principle behind inner peace and contentment which leads to creativity. Being mindful means giving full concentration to whatsoever we are doing in the present, having no real awareness of anything else, becoming completely absorbed, lost in the activity and the moment. According to Clare (2003), "this experience of the moment means that we are far more likely to notice things around us...." This suggests that intuition, creativity, and inspiration come to a person only through such a state of 'extraordinary' mind. Perhaps, this is the reason why the stage of "illumination" comes in the process of creative thinking only after the stages of preparation and incubation.

Wisdom

Many cultures assume that as people grow older, they gain in wisdom—insight and judgement about many practical matters and life problems. Thus, whatsoever happens to reaction time, memory, or even fluid intelligence, individuals become more valuable members of society as a result of their accumulated wisdom. Sternberg (2003), however, views wisdom "as the value-laden application of tacit knowledge not only for one's own benefit (as can be the case with successful intelligence) but also for the benefit of others, in order to attain a common good. The wise person realizes that what matters is not just knowledge, or the intellectual skills one applies to this knowledge, but how the knowledge is used." Therefore, his Balance Theory of Wisdom maintains that wisdom is the balancing interests of successful intelligence and creativity. It is an art of maintaining balance among self-interest (intrapersonal), someone else's interest (interpersonal) and other aspects of the contexts in which he/she lives (extra-personal) over short and long terms. Thus, it is not just maximizing self-interest or interest of the organization but also seeking good outcomes for others. This is the reason why people in the East are taught the meaning of life and become *karmyogis* concentrating on their energies on actions having no expectations about the results of their labour. And they are also made to realize that such fruits (results) flow only from the Divine Hand.

This kind of wisdom, therefore, gives us the insight to make a divine distinction between cause and effect. Today, many persons grapple most of the time with the effects, without understanding the causes. As a result, they fail to provide permanent solutions and problems crop up again and again in different forms. Since we are conditioned to think in a particular way—with the aid of hardened logic—we cannot get the subtle truth. We, therefore, need to develop an intuitive ability of wisdom to understand the subtlety of truth. Siddiqui (2005) has rightly said that "those who heed ancient wisdom and cosmic principles will emerge as winners in new age."

Thus, successful intelligence and creativity, though necessary, are not sufficient conditions for wisdom. We need to develop it separately. For this, we need to learn:

1. How to maintain balance between the two, and
2. How to change our ordinary mind to extraordinary mind through spiritual development.

References

Baron, R.A. (1995). *Psychology.* New Delhi: Prentice-Hall of India.

Cattell, R.B. (1963). Theory of fluid and crystallized intelligence: A critical experiment. *Journal of Educational Psychology*, 54, 1-22.

Clare, S. (2003). *Trust your intuition* (2nd ed.). Delhi: Macmillan.

Cattell, R.B. (1987). *Intelligence: Its structure, growth and action.* Amsterdam: North Holland.

Das, J.P. (1998). *The working mind.* New Delhi: Sage.

Fitz, H.K. (2001). *Intuition: Its nature and usage in human experience.* Delhi: Motilal Banarsidass.

Isen, A.M. & Baron, R.A. (1991). Positive effect and organizational behaviour. In B.M. Staw the L.L. Cummings (Eds.). *Research in organizational behaviour.* (Vol. 14, pp. 1-48), Greenwich, CT: JAI Press.

Schank, R. (1988). *The creating attitude.* New York: Macmillan.

Siddiqui, M. (2005). *Corporate soul.* New Delhi: Response Books (Sage).

Spearman, C. (1927). *The abilities of man.* London: Macmillan.

Sternberg, R.J. (2003). *Wisdom, intelligence, and creativity synthesized.* Cambridge: Cambridge University Press.

Thurstone, L.L. (1938). Primary mental abilities. *Psychometric Monograph*, No. 1.

3

Eastern and Western Approaches to Love and Spirituality in Management

(Paper presented at International Conference on "Expanding Horizons of Indian Business Management" organized by Indian Business Academy, Bangalore from January 15 to 16, 2008)

Recently all managers—Eastern and Western—have started showing good interest in integrating spirituality and management. Their interest is important because for them integrating the two brings profound meanings in their jobs and lives. It brings their deepest values to bear on their work and a promise of success and fulfilment. As a result, they are feeling today more concerned towards their employees and are showing 'genuine love' for them. This kind of love is not about romance or sex but about genuine compassion for human kind. This love is also not referring to any God or religion, as many religions do, but to the quality of human existence, personal values and beliefs, interpersonal relationships, connection to the natural world, and beyond (Heyn, Stojanovic, and Talwar,

2006). This kind of feeling has made many of the managers to perceive love and spirituality as the same thing. However, these two are two different things but playing very, very important roles in management and business today.

What is Love?

Of all the emotions associated with close relationships, love is the most central for people in many cultures. But the word "love" can describe a wide variety of thoughts, feelings and behaviours, including, among others, fondness, passion, adoration, admiration, enhancement, desire, longing, attachment, yearning and sex. For two persons who love each other, however, love may not mean exactly the same thing because they might be experiencing love in different ways.

Love binds us together as husbands and wives, parents and children, friends and neighbours, teachers and students. Its importance can hardly be overrated. Therefore, an English writer, Robert Burton has rightly said that '*no cord or cable can so forcibly draw, or hold so fast, as love can do with a twined thread.*' It is thus both a feeling and an activity. A person feels love for someone and acts in a loving manner.

But we can also be angry with the person we love. This is the paradox of love: it encompasses opposites. It includes affection and anger, excitement and boredom, stability and change, bond and freedom. Therefore, Lee (1988) has rightly said that studying love is no guarantee of finding it. Perhaps this is the reason why love has emerged as a "triangle" in the Western laboratory—the three sides being physiological, psychological, and anthropological. But, outside the laboratory, particularly in India, the "true love" has emerged as a "circle" which combines all the three components into one. This combination as a whole is known as "spiritual love" in which all the three components are merged with each other in an appropriate (balanced) proportion.

What is Spirituality?

Spirituality appears to be an integral part of all cultures. Spiritual development may be regarded as connection with something external to the self, or as an internal experience, or both. According to Clark (1958), Spirituality can be most characteristically described as "the inner experience of the individual when he senses a Beyond, especially as evidenced by the effect of this experience on his behaviour when he actively attempts to harmonize his life with the Beyond." The Beyond includes unusual varieties of human experience, including the ability to create relationships with what are perceived to be Gods, spirits, ancestors, or other non-physical realities. Spiritual evolution thus can be assessed as "*ability to channel esoteric information.*"

Indian thinkers are of the firm opinion that every human behaviour has three aspects—*the physical*, *the mental*, and *the spiritual*. The spiritual aspect may be difficult to define exactly. However, for those who believe in Gestalt psychology, it is not that difficult to explain or experience. Gestaltists maintain that the whole is more than the sum total of its parts. Since every human behaviour has minimum two parts (it is partly mental and partly physical), as a whole, it results in something more than that (spiritual). This Gestalt effect, however, will appear better only when mind and body interact in appropriate proportion without dominating upon each other. This becomes the best combination and makes the behaviour highly effective or spiritual.

The New Age Management consultants, therefore, are deriving management principles from such Eastern mystical groups and not from *Harvard Business Review*. They recommend working in a meditative state of consciousness (making work a form of service) because they find that their relationship with God influences their work lives more than any other factor (McCormick, 1994). Hoffman (2002) has also indicated that "In coming years, we'll surely see scientific validation on the connection between our spiritual well-being at work and our highest productivity involving both mind and body." Science, religion and spirituality are thus strongly influencing many managers' behaviour today at work. In view of all these, it can be safely concluded that, if managers want to be successful, they need to learn how to synthesize science, religion, and spirituality.

Synthesis of Science, Religion, and Spirituality

Science, religion, and spirituality are certainly the most three forces that have shaped the course of humanity. In spite of an atmosphere of indifference and occasional rivalry, many eminent thinkers, including scientists as well as theologians, have deeply pondered over the close relationship among these three disciplines and have felt the need for a synthesis among them to answer many complex problems of human life.

To satisfy the conditions of the scientific method, a scientist follows certain scientific principles demonstrating under a given set of conditions. This simple rule has allowed science to progress and mature into a powerful system for understanding our world around. This rule, however, has restricted scientists to study only those phenomena which are "external" to human consciousness, and which can be observed through five sense organs. But what about those experiences which are "internal" to human consciousness and are behind the five senses? At this juncture, religion and spirituality are coming forward as balancing forces to promote understanding and importance of "internal" experiences. This is a natural application for religion and spirituality, where a group of people gather together, validate their internal experiences (but never bother to verify), find strength and respect for each other, and then face worlds with renewed determination.

But again the question arises: why both, religion and spirituality; why not only one? The answer is simple. Many definitions of spirituality have come from the concept of religion. However, these two are not synonymous. Religion is a way of life which has been put in the mind of every person by socialization process. This has become a part of his/her personality and a ritual to follow. Therefore, Conger (1994), drawing from Roof's research (1993), says that religion has an institutional connotation which means practicing rituals, adhering to dogma, and attending services. Spirituality, on the other hand, has more to do with life's deeper motivations and an emotional connotation to God. An Indian Visionary Saint, Srila Prabhupada, the Founder Acharya of the Bhaktivedanta Institute for a Synthesis of Science and Spirituality, has rightly commented that "Human intellect is developed for advancement of learning in art, science, philosophy, physics, chemistry, psychology, economics, politics, etc. By culture of such knowledge the human society can attain perfection of life." And this culture of such knowledge in the service of God is known as spirituality.

Importance of Spirituality in Management

Today, many of the organizations are run by emotionally immature persons because they find certain positive correlations between aggression (which creates fear) and outcomes. Perhaps, this is the reason why many of the B-Schools are also teaching about how to be "aggressive". But they forget that such results are only temporary and at the cost of healthy relationships between management and employees. Not only that, in order to achieve targets, some employees are also encouraged to use unfair means. Therefore, managers need to learn about how to achieve long-term results and how to maintain long-term relationships with the employees. For this, the only way is to align work and organizations with some of the most basic human needs—to be loved and to find our own purpose and meaningful connections in life. It has been rightly pointed out by Heyn, Stojanovic, and Talwar (2006) that "For a hundred years or more, millions upon millions of people who need love and spiritual meaning like they need food and drink, are denied these basic life requirements at a place that occupies the majority of their useful existence (their work), because love and spirituality (and all that these words represent) seemingly don't feature on the corporate agenda."

These authors have said very nicely in their article, "*Love and spirituality in management and business*" that today many persons are fed up with the selfish character of corporations and organizations and the way they conduct themselves with the help of technology and worldwide web. Customers also feel that they are cheated by these organizations through their advertisements and slogans. As a result, every staff and customer is looking for a change. In such situation, the only hope left to these managers and leaders is to take care of the people and the planet—and not to make just profit and exploit them for personal gains. And 'proper care of the people and the planet' is possible only through love, compassion, and spirituality. It is good that the importance of all these are being realized today and things have started changing.

Comparison Between Eastern and Western Approaches

One of the greatest contributions of India to the world is the *Bhagavad Gita* which is the essence of the *Vedas* and *Upanishads*. It is a universal scripture applicable to people of all temperaments and for all times. It is a book with sublime thoughts and practical instructions on Yoga, Devotion, Vedanta and Action. The management lessons of this holy book have been brought into lights by many, many persons including Maharshi Mahesh Yogi, Adi Sankaracharya, Sri Srila Prabhupada Swami, Sri Aurobindo, Swami Vivekananda, Sri Shri Ravi Shankar (Bhattathiri, 2006). As a result, today every Indian is known as a born philosopher throughout the world. Therefore, we must try to understand what guidelines this holy book offers to managers.

In modern management, which is primarily Western, the whole emphasis is laid on the management of externals like people, organization, material, and environment. But the Eastern spiritual thinkers have repeatedly pointed out that right management of the internal self is the key to the successful management of the outer life and environment. Someone who cannot manage his/her own self, cannot effectively manage others. Therefore, Self-management is the key to Life-management. And Self-management, according to Sri Aurobindo (Gupta, 2004), starts with: *Know Thyself* which includes *Know Your Mind*, *Change Yourself*, *Maintain Good Relationship with Others*, and *Learn to Concentrate*, etc. The moment a person starts this kind of inward journey, he/she starts having spiritual evolution and getting all these automatically because all are available in his/her mind. "There is a genius within everyone of us—we don't know it. We must find the way to make it come out—but it is there sleeping, it asks for nothing better than to manifest; we must open the door to it" (Gupta, 2004).

According to Vedanta, the conscious mind is known as *antahkarana* (internal instrument) which perceives things through five sense organs and acts through five organs of action. The power of consciousness, however, is not the built-in characteristic of the mind. This comes from some higher source known as Soul, Atman or Self. Since mind is not the real perceiver or knower of the mental phenomena—as claimed by Western psychologists, Vedanta differentiates between the mind and the Self—the mind as an object (the known) and the Self as a subject (the knower). Thus, the ultimate observer or experiencer is the Self, not the mind (Ellis, 1994). Mind is simply functioning like a mirror which can perceive clearly only when it is fully illuminated by the Soul. Since Soul, like sun, is throwing lights constantly on the mirror, it is for the mind to absorb it properly. If it is neat and clean, it will absorb better, and thereby perceive better. In this sense, Vedanta rightly says that it is possible for us to make our conscious mind "Superconscious" which can perceive things in a far better way making use of all the informations available in the so called subconscious and unconscious minds. Superconscious Mind is thus such a state of mind which experiences cosmic connectivity and has clear understanding, peace, wisdom and enlightenment (Sharan, 2007). This is the reason why Sri Aurobindo says to learn about *Know Thyself* first before knowing about others.

The second important thing is: *Do Karmas.* For many of the Western researchers, human action is just a behaviour. But for Indian thinkers, it is more than that—"*karma*"—which refers to one's intention or motivation while doing an action. According to Tsering (2004), intention is the most important of all mental events because it gives direction to the mind, determining whether we engage in virtuous, non-virtuous, or neutral objects. Just as iron is powerlessly drawn to a magnet, our minds are powerlessly drawn to the object of our intentions. Intention may be expressed through either physical or verbal actions. Actually, Indian thinkers differentiate between human and animal behaviours. They argue that in the case of animals, instinct prevails, but in the case of human beings, reason prevails. Therefore, only human beings, not animals, have the freedom and capacity to judge rightly or wrongly about their behaviours (actions). This exercise of judgement is known as *karma* and this makes human life as the *karma-bhumi.* The Holy Gita, therefore, puts maximum emphasis on this aspect and teaches management students to realize its importance. Not only that, the Gita also explains further how we are all governed by the universal *Karmic Law:* "As you sow, so you reap." Therefore, understanding of this *Karmic Law* and practicing accordingly is a must for all managers. Otherwise, life-long we shall go on suffering and shall never enjoy happiness in true sense.

The third important lesson given by this holy book is: *Remain Detached.* Western thinkers have been putting maximum emphasis on motivation and involvement and have been recommending celebration of success. But Eastern thinkers have been pleading for just reverse *(nishkama karma):* remaining detached from the fruits or results of the actions performed. Being dedicated to work is itself more than enough because it creates excellence, and there is no need to feel excited about it. Spiritual laws say that the moment a person is feeling excited and/or highly motivated, his/her mind is not able to concentrate properly on a task. As a result, the outcomes get either delayed or become negative. Therefore, we need to do our *karmas* with all honesty and sincerity without expecting or worrying for the outcomes because they are always decided by our God. Indian thinkers also add here that even if God decides something unfavourably, it goes in favour of the person—if not today, tomorrow. The person should simply learn to appreciate His wish. Bhattathiri (2006) has rightly quoted from what Sri Krishna says in the 10th Chapter of the Gita that "I am the strength of those who are devoid of personal desire and attachment. O Arjuna, I am the legitimate desire in those, who are not opposed to righteousness."

To sum up, it can be concluded that we must find a way to lead our business life in harmony with our inner life. All sincere managers, therefore, need to learn how to integrate their inner lives with their outward actions. Without finding a place of balance, a harmony between the 'spiritual' and the 'secular', or the outer and the inner, we will experience frustration and disappointment.

References

Bhattathiri, M.P., (2006). *Spirituality and management.* www.worldspirituality.org/spirituality—management.html

Clark, W.H., (1958). *The psychology of religion.* New York: Macmillan.

Conger, J.A., (1994). Our search for spiritual community. In J.A. Conger and Associates. *Spirit at work: Discovering the spirituality in leadership.* San Francisco, CA: Jossey-Bass.

Ellis, R. (Ed). (1994). *Mind according to Vedanta.* Madras: Sri Ramkrishna Math.

Gupta, G.P., (2004). *Towards holistic management.* Pondicherry: Sri Aurobindo Society.

Heyn, Barbara, Stojanovic, Sonia & Talwar, Charu, (2006). *Love and spirituality in management and business.* www.businessballs.com/love.htm

Hoffman, E., (2002). *Psychological testing at work.* New York: McGraw Hill.

Lee, J.A., (1988). "Love styles". In R.J. Sternberg the M.L. Barnes (Eds.), *The psychology of love.* New Haven, CT: Yale University Press.

McCormick, D.W., (1994). Spirituality and management. *Journal of Managerial Psychology*, 9 (6).

Roof, W.C., (1993). *A generation of speakers: The spiritual journey of the Baby Boom generation.* San Francisco, CA: Harper Collins.

Sharan, M.B., (2007). Making psychology complete and essential for understanding of the human mind, behaviour and intuitive awareness. *Psychological Studies*, 52 (3).

Tsering, G.T., (2004). *The Buddha's medicine for the mind: Cultivating wisdom and compassion.* South Mellbourne, Vic.: Lothian Books.

4

Dreams as a Guide to Our Meaningful Life

(Special Lecture delivered at 17th Annual Conference of the National Academy of Psychology held at IIT, Kanpur from December 17 to 19, 2007)

The Nature of Dreams

A dream is an illusory psychic activity, particularly of a visual nature which occurs during sleep. It is essentially a psychological phenomenon with many philosophical, religious and moral implications. It can be natural or supernatural. If they are supernatural, their origin lies in soul or God. Dreams are so complex that what causes them can seldom be traced back to a well-defined external or internal stimulus (Augustine, 1996). They are perhaps brought about by many interacting factors of a perceptual, emotional, motivational, devotional, and physiological nature. They occur in cycles following the fluctuation of sleep stages. As suggested by some of the researches, generally, a person dreams for 1 to 2 hours distributed in three to five periods lasting from 20 to 30 minutes, and each sleep period followed at intervals of about 90 minutes.

We all dream but we do not remember all of them. And those we remember are also full of confusions. Only some dreams we find to be somewhat meaningful and associated with our memories and experiences of that day or of the past. This is the reason why Jacobson (1999) has said that (i) there is no dream without nonsense, and (ii) there are some in a form of prophecy. But the real problem is how to distinguish between the two. Since it is all bundled into one snowball, the question is: how to interpret which part is meaningless and which part is meaningful.

Beginning of the Systematic Study

A dream is a glimpse into the subconscious or unconscious mind which functions differently from the conscious mind. Therefore, we cannot expect dreams to be systematic and logical. Moreover, when we try to interpret dreams, we try to do so through our conscious mind. As a result, dreams remain distant and illogical hallucinatory experiences most of the times. Credit goes to Freud that he kept the conscious mind in the background and interpreted dreams with whole emphasis on the unconscious mind. This led him to say that dreams were meaningful and attempted with fulfilment of unsatisfied desires. In his book, *Interpretation of Dreams* he argued that the unconscious mind liked to depict the wish fulfilment in wholesale but the preconscious could not allow it. As a result, the wish or wishes remained disguised within a dream. He further claimed that the counterintuitive nature of nightmares represented a clash between the *super ego* and the *id*—the id wished to see the past fulfilled, while the super ego could not allow it. He also added that in nearly all cases these anxiety dreams were products of infantile, sexual memories (Wikipedia, 2007). Dreams were thus "a tree for secret erotic desires, a hat for oedipal tendencies, a pillar for adultery, a bird for a phallic symbol in Freudian interpretation" (Bhattacharya, 2000).

Freud's student-turned rebel, Jung, however, did not agree with his teacher, and proposed many things additional. He believed that during the Rapid Eye Movement (REM) state, the mind got in touch with the unconscious, which consisted of not only the 'personal unconscious'—with its repressed desires and fears—but also the racial memories and experiences of the 'collective unconscious'. He further maintained that the interpretation of dreams was largely based on the personality and circumstances of the dreamer. The general function of dream was thus "to try to restore our psychological balance" in Jung's writings (Bhattacharya, 2000). Adler also saw this past, present, and future influence on dreams. His main contention was, however, to interpret how a person's lifestyle was reflected in his/her dreams.

Present Status of Dreams

Everyone will agree that Freud and Jung were the two masterminds in the field of dream analysis. Jung, however, had an edge over Freud. Agreeing with his teacher reluctantly, Jung was also pointing out his missing points that dreams represented the various layers of the mind and contained ineluctable truths, philosophical pronouncements, illusions, wild fantasies, memories, plans, irrational experiences, and telepathic visions. Today, many of the researches are supporting Jung by saying that dreams have an almost unlimited source of creative inspiration, psychological insight, and spiritual guidance. Researches on brain are also showing that when a person falls asleep, he/she has a steady pattern of alpha waves on the electroencephalograph (EEG). "These are accompanied by regular breathing, slow pulse rate, and a drop in the body temperature. This is the non-REM sleep. In the REM state, dreams occur four to five times a night. REM is also marked by intense motor activity, increased pulse rate, and a brain pattern similar to alert wakefulness" (Bhattacharya, 2000).

Kaplan (2002) has elaborated these different stages of dreams in her book, *Dreams are Letters from the Soul* very nicely. She says that the first stage of dreaming is directional, goal-oriented, with a more masculine feel. In this stage, we discern and integrate information about the dreamer. In the second stage, which is spherical, spiralling and receptive, we learn to access and decode information that lies beyond our individual awareness. These collective nature of the dreams include the telepathic (information about something that is happening or has just occurred), clairvoyant (awareness of an immediate future possibility), and prophetic (awareness of a distant future possibility) experiences. The third stage dreams are transformative which include healing, teaching and oracular dreams. This stage of dreaming is a sacred marriage of the first two stages—a coming together of our directional and goal-oriented dreams with our receptive dreams. The fourth stage dreaming is what the author calls "philanthropic" dreams in which a person can "work" through the dream world, in complete service to others. Most people will reach this stage only after years of spiritual work, both in the dream space and in waking life (Denwiddie, 2003). Thus, according to Kaplan, "Our sleep is not merely a time for decreased consciousness and rest. It is a time to awaken to the collective conscious of the soul, to communicate with our Creator. Let us use them to help us become truly awakened, that we may be used to awaken others."

Michaels (2005) has also written in her book, *A Bedside Guide to Dreams* that both insights and meanings emerge in our dreams. "Remember, dreams are letters from your soul, not generally meant to simply entertain you. Under most circumstances, applying the dream's insight will produce a constructive change in you as you align yourself more closely with your soul's purpose." After documenting 27 types of dreams, she summarized that dreams were related to the following six basic life issues:

1. *Body and Health:* When we learn to pay attention to our dreams, we realize that we have our own built-in doctor. Sometimes when we dream that certain foods disagree with our body, we also see how to heal ourselves.
2. *Relationships:* Very often, our dreams give us feedback about our behaviour in the relationship and how to clear up our acts to make room for a better relationship.
3. *Decision-making:* Decision-making dreams do not give direct answers to our problems but offer a clearer view of the situations, which can help in taking right decisions.
4. *Male and Female Balancing:* We may see ourselves doing something that is not characteristic of us but the opposite trait needs to be brought in for maintaining balance.
5. *Strength:* Strength dreams act like meters to show us the level of strength or vulnerability we are feeling.
6. *Sex:* Sometimes we have sex dreams as a way of balancing our own sexual energy or resolving our psychological feelings about sexuality.

Thus, many of the researchers (e.g. Thurston, 1978; Bhattacharya, 2000; Todeschi, 2002, 2004; Reed, 2003; Holloway, 2006) are of the opinion today that dreams do not come unbidden or without purpose. They come to help us in some way. They do this by having us reach beyond our individuality into timelessness and spacelessness. We, therefore, need to realize that all parts of the mind (conscious, subconscious and unconscious) merge in dreams into one and become universal to give us a window view of our soul (Michaels, 2005).

Creating Meaningful Dreams

We have seen that dreams occur in cycles in different stages. The first stage dream, which is directional and which is more concerned with dreamer's unsatisfied desires, perhaps comes at its own. Therefore, many of us experience such dreams as wish fulfilment of the day-to-day desires as claimed by Freud in his first theory of dream interpretation. But when we go deeper and deeper into our unconscious mind to have second, third or fourth stage dream, we find them changing in many ways—becoming more and more informative, constructive, meaningful and prophetic. Dreams of such stages, however, appear only in such persons who want to have them and also want to remember them. Otherwise, only some persons can experience even second and third stage dream and that also occasionally. Kaplan (2002) has rightly said that people can have third and fourth stage dreams (prophetic and philanthropic) only after years of spiritual work in both the dream space and waking life. Michaels (2005), therefore, has suggested the following steps to remember dreams and to reach the fourth stage:

1. *Get a Note Book:* You may find that you will recall your dreams better when you record them in the note book. And the words you choose to describe dreams also give you an insight to what the dreams mean later on.

2. *Relax Before you Retire:* By relaxing beforehand, you allow your psyche to shift gears away from the outward, and enter into the inner role-oriented public life you want to lead.
3. *Notice What is on your Mind:* If you are aware of your thoughts and feelings just before you go to sleep, you may find yourself halfway to interpreting your dreams when you awake.
4. *Don't Forget to Give Yourself a Suggestion:* "I will remember my dreams" may suffice, or you may wish to pray for guidance, or understanding a particular dream.
5. *Wake up Comfortably:* Try to wake up at your own by giving suggestions to your mind. If you use an alarm clock, use a soft one with quiet music.
6. *Don't Move too Abruptly:* It is difficult to hold onto the thin, filmy material of the unconscious. A quick movement, even a stretch as you lay in bed can plant you firmly in the conscious world, only with a wisp of feeling that you had some great and important dream.

Comparison Between Eastern and Western Thinkers

Bhattacharya (2000) has examined the views of some of the Indian researchers in her article elaborately. We find that the world of dreams has been a mystery for many of them. Therefore, each one has been interpreting dreams in his/her own way. There was a time when many were holding the view that during sleep the soul of a person was coming out and wandering here and there, and was having all sorts of experiences known as dreams. Today, however, there is a shift in their thinking. For some, it is a reflection of repressed desires; for some, it is a desire of the *jiva* (individual consciousness) to merge with *Shiva* (cosmic consciousness). "The Indian tradition believes that the pre-dawn moment is the *Brahama muhurat* or *Brahama time*. When the last stars are still twinkling in the sky, a window opens in the cosmic consciousness and reaches out to the individual consciousness" (Bhattacharya, 2000). This results in prophetic dreams in some devoted persons. Thus, Bhattacharya and some other Indian thinkers have been considering dreams to be prophetic in nature (like "letters from the soul"). They have not been, however, talking about other stages of dreaming as Kaplan (2002) is saying today which seems to be more logical and convincing.

There is another similarity between Eastern and Western thinkers. Both the groups have been saying that lucid dreaming is possible only by affirming again and again by the dreamer that he/she wants to have meaningful dreams. Unless a person gives importance to such dreams, it is not possible for him or her to have it. Castaneda (1993) has rightly said in his book, *The Art of Dreaming* that dreaming is an art of shifting our assemblage point—a point of brilliance inside the energy field of human body. "The greater the displacement, the more unusual the dream." Thus, according to him, nothing is impossible in the dream world, if a person wishes genuinely. Wahiduddin (2005) has also written in his article, *In an Eastern Rose Garden* that mastery lies not merely in stilling the mind, but in directing it towards whatever point we desire, in allowing it to be active as far as we wish, in using it to fulfil our purpose, in causing it to be still when we want to still it.

Sri Aurobindo in India presented a similar view during Jung's lifetime. He said that dreams could be classified as those occurring on the subconscious levels and those occurring on the corresponding but the higher levels of consciousness ("subliminal" or "supraconscious" levels). "All the subconscious level dreams will be composed of various impressions from the environment or physical nature and from deeper levels of the subconscious related to the personal and collective past. The supraconscious dreams are due to activities of our higher levels of being, involving perceptions or experiences.... These levels of consciousness are seen as the origins of inspirations, creativity, intuitions, ideas, will-suggestions, sense-suggestions, and urges to action."

Thus, many of the great Indian thinkers have been thinking about dreams to be a feedback mechanism of our subconscious mind and Higher Self from the very beginning which the Western researchers are emphasizing today after so many years of research. They were, however, not accounting dreams stage-by-stage as these researchers are presenting today.

Critical Evaluation and Conclusion

From the above discussion, it is clear that every person is dreaming almost every night. It is another thing that many of them don't remember them because they don't have the intention to remember. Similarly, even if they remember some, they don't give much importance to their dreams. Therefore, for them, dreams appear to be meaningless. Otherwise, any person who wants to remember his/her dreams can remember them and can find meanings in them. Stone (2004) has rightly written in his article, *A Spiritual Perspective on Dreams and Sleep* that since for the Senoi Indians, dreams are more important than their real lives, every morning upon rising they are sharing their dreams with each other as a sacred ritual.

Dreams are definitely complex in nature. We, therefore, need to understand how our subconscious and unconscious minds function during sleep and how our conscious mind interprets them in the morning on awakening. For this, first of all, we need to understand: (i) what is mind? and (ii) how does it matter for dreams? Though mind has been defined in many ways by different authors, an appropriate definition has come from Vedanta. It maintains that mind is like an internal instrument which is getting the power of consciousness from soul. And it is functioning like a mirror which can perceive things clearly only when it is neat and clean. Soul is like the sun which is throwing lights on it constantly. Now, it depends on the absorbing ability of the mind that how much it gets illuminated. Only a well-illuminated mind can have correct perceptions and decisions; otherwise, it will have distorted perceptions. Since there are layers in it, from functional viewpoint, psychologists have divided it into three parts: conscious, subconscious, and unconscious. Otherwise, as a whole, these three parts constitute one mind best known as Superconscious or Universal Mind—Superconscious because consciousness comes from the soul and Universal because it has infinite intelligence. This Universal Mind is thus functioning like a mega computer that orchestrates the activities in every little computer of conscious, subconscious and unconscious minds connected to it (Reed, 1989; Koh, 2004; Sharan, 2007).

During sleep, the mind gets a chance to function better because the person is at rest and dreaming. It is not possible for the person to have this kind of mind when he/she is awaken (except in meditation) because it is actively involved in day-to-day problems dealing with anxieties and worries. But the moment a person goes to bed, he/she starts feeling relaxed and at peace. This allows the person to go deeper and deeper into his/her mind and have all sorts of dreams, including prophetic dreams. Wahiduddin (2005) has rightly said that "The mind has no leisure; it is perhaps worrying, or planning, or thinking over the struggles and anxieties of which life is so full. There is hardly ever a time when the mind is at rest, except when nature gives it a rest because it is too exhausted to work anymore." This is the time when mind says, 'I will have a good sleep.'

For prophetic dreams, however, a good sleep is not enough. It needs to function in a particular direction to go deeper and deeper and to have more and more meaningful dreams. Therefore, the person needs to have a genuine interest at his/her conscious level first to have meaningful dreams. This kind of intention and expectation prepares the subconscious and unconscious mind to have incubating dreams of the second and third stage. Thus, only in the case of strong desire to have prophetic dreams, the dreamer reaches the fourth stage and has prophetic dreams. Actually, this kind of request or instructions to the conscious mind conveys a message to the subconscious and unconscious minds to find out something meaningful by filtering the dreams. This process of filtering thus changes the dream pattern from one stage to another and is successful finally in having prophetic dreams of the fourth stage. Wahiduddin (2005), therefore, has rightly suggested that unless the mind is directed to find out meanings in dreams, it cannot do it at its own.

Secondly, a good sleep starts with the first stage dream of personal nature including satisfaction of some of the unsatisfied desires of the dreamer. Then, in second stage, the dreamer has a different kind of dream which is more concerned with the information that lies beyond his/her awareness. Then, if sleep is uninterrupted, the dreamer experiences third stage dream which is of transformative nature—saying more about solving a difficult problem. Then, when the dreamer's mind is fully (spiritually) prepared, it enters into the fourth and final stage where he/she has prophetic and philanthropic dreams which reflect more about future of the dreamer. Since a person is reaching the Universal Mind only in this stage, it becomes possible for him or to her to glimpse spiritual and moral possibilities hidden in it only in this (fourth) stage. According to Ellis (1994), "It holds possibilities which are locked away from the conscious mind, for it has at its disposal all subliminal psychic contents, all those things which have been forgotten or overlooked, as well as the wisdom and experience of uncounted centuries which are laid down in its archetypal organs...." J. Krishnamurti is also of the same opinion that "In oneself lies the whole world and if you know to look and learn, then the door is there and the key is in your hands. Nobody on earth can give you either the key or the door to open, except yourself." All of us, therefore, need to learn how to have such dreams to reach the Universal Mind and to know the "whole world". Michaels (2005) has already given steps to remember dreams and to reach the fourth stage. However, the most important thing in this context is what Kaplan has said that people can have third and fourth stage dreams (prophetic and philanthropic) only after years of spiritual work in both the dream space and waking life. This includes repeated affirmation and prayer by the dreamer that he/she wants to have meaningful dreams.

Thirdly, for understanding such prophetic dreams meaningfully, we need to learn about the art of interpreting them. Scientific methods have not been found to be of much use in this regard. Psychologists, therefore, need to realize the limitations of their experimental and other methods which can explore only up to REM and some other physiological changes involved in dreams. But for getting hidden meanings in dreams, they have to change their mindsets and have to accept Intuition as a method of psychology. This is the reason why many Indian thinkers like Dr. S. Radhakrishnan

(McDermott, 1970), Swami Vivekananda (2005), Sri Aurobindo (1996) have been pleading strongly for having Intuitive Awareness for getting truth. The same view is now being supported by many Western psychologists like Thurston (1978), Todeschi (2002, 2004), Seale (2002), Reed (2002) etc. It has been rightly said that without following Intuition, intellectuals will remain imperfect and divided, and blind to the truth behind appearances. According to Swami Omkarananda (1999), "Intuition is the only way by which Absolute can be realized and experienced in all its totality. The mortal, finite, limited senses and the intellect cannot comprehend the Reality which is immortal and all-pervading."

Not only dreams, psychologists can also understand topics like love, trust, confidence, concentration, creativity, spirituality, wisdom, etc. better by accepting Intuition as a method of psychology. Since they are trained to address only such questions which can be tested in a precise, objective, and publicly verifiable fashion, they are unable to capture these topics. But once they come out of such mindsets, they will enjoy Intuitive Awareness of all these topics including dreams. All of us, therefore, need to realize the limitations of our methods, which offer only a few subjective and objective factors, involved in each of these topics but not the "Gestalt effect" created by these factors. Only through Intuitive Awareness this Gestalt effect (as a whole effect) can be appreciated which is full of spiritual meanings in each of these topics including dreams. These spiritual meanings actually serve as a guide to one's meaningful life. Ashish (2007) has rightly said that "Movement on the spiritual path necessarily involves taking light into the dark corner of our psyche, and it is there that dreams provide an open window into the inner reality.

References

Ashish, M. (2007). *An open window: Dreams as everyone's guide to spirit*.http://www.penguinbooksindia.com/Books/prnbookdetail.asp/=6537

Augustine, Fr. (1996). *Dreams.* http://www.ewtn.com/library/SPIRIT/DREAMS.TXT

Aurobindo, Sri. (1996). *Lights on yoga* (4th impression). Pondicherry: Sri Aurobindo Ashram.

Bhattacharya, A. (2000). *Dream works.* http:www.life positive.com/paranormal/dreams/ dream.asp

Castaneda, C. (1993). *The art of dreaming.* New York: Harper Collins Publishers.

Coleman, J.E. (2000). *The quiet mind.* New Delhi: New Age Books.

Denwiddie, VirDella. (2003). *Book summary of A bedside guide to* dreams. http://www.intuitiveconnections.net.2003/bookbedside dreams.htm

Ellis, R. (Ed.). (1994). *Mind: According to Vedanta.* Madras: Sri Ramakrishna Math.

Holloway, G. (2006). *The complete dream book.* Illinois: Source Books. Inc.

Jacobson, S. (1999). *Toward a meaningful life with Simon Jacobson* (Radio Show Transcript). www.meaningfullife.com

Kaplan, C. (2002). *Dreams are letters from the souls.* New York: Harmony Books.

Koh, K. (2004). *Mind power explained.* http://www.subconscioussecrets.com

McDermott, R.A. (Ed.). (1970). *Basic writings of S. Radhakrishnan.* Bombay: Jaico Publishing House.

Michaels, S. (2005). *A bedside guide to dreams.* http://www.intuitive-connections.net/2005/book—bedsudedreams.htm

Omkarananda, Swami. (1999). *The intuitive experience of the truth.* www.omkarananda-ashram.net/intuitive.html

Reed, H. (1989). *Edgar Cayce on mysteries of the mind.* New York: Warner Books.

Reed, H. (2002). *Receiving intuitive guidance in dreams.* http:// www.intuitive-connections.net/eciis-dreams.htm

Reed, H. (2003). *Incubating dreams solve problems.* http:// www.intuitive-connections.net/2003/dreamincubation.htm

Seale, A. (2002). *Intuitive living.* New Delhi: New Age Books.

Sharan, M.B. (2005). Understanding of human mind and behaviour: The missing link of intuitive experience. *Psychological Studies*, 50, 259-262.

Sharan, M.B. (2007). *Making psychology complete and essential for understanding the human of mind, behaviour and intuitive awareness.* http://www.intuitive-connections.net/2007/sharan/htm

Stone, J.D. (2004). *A spiritual perspective on dreams and sleep.* http:// www.iamuniversity.org

Thurston, M.A. (1978). *How to interpret your dreams.* Virginia Beach: A.R.E. Press.

Todeschi, K. (2002). *Dream interpretation (and more) made easy.* http://www.paraview.com/ todeschi/todeschi_excerpt.htm

Todeschi, K. (2004). *Dream images and symbols.* Virginia Beach: A.R.E. Press.

Vivekananda, Swami. (2005). *Powers of the mind* (24th Impression). Kolkata: Advaita Ashram.

Wahiduddin, R.S. (2005). *Stilling the mind.* http://wahiduddin.net/ mv2/VII/VII_16.htm

Wikipedia, the free encyclopedia. (2007). *Dream interpretation.* http://en.wikipedia.org/ wiki/Dream_interpretation.

5

Universal Laws of Karma and Reincarnation

Evidences for Life After Death

Is there life after death? And, if it is, what is the evidence for that? These questions have been asked by many persons very often. This can be answered only when we know what someone means by the term "evidence". If he or she is looking for "scientific" evidence, then perhaps nobody can satisfy him or her. But if he/she is ready to realize that life after death (reincarnation) is a metaphysical reality (meta means "beyond" and physical means "material"), then many convincing evidences can be cited in its favour. The subject of reincarnation has been examined by many persons from different countries from different angles and has been accepted today beyond any doubt (Stevenson, 1974; Khoo, 1995; Chadwick, 1988; Knapp, 2005; Sivananda, 2001; Abhedananda, 2007; Yogananda, 2007). Therefore, we should look for those evidences first to understand the existence of reincarnation. We should not forget that the modern psychology has the dual roots of philosophy and science and its scope has broadened considerably in recent years to include non-material things like mind, experience, soul, love, and spirituality in it. There was a time when Watson wanted to make psychology a 'natural' science and was not in favour of accepting anything of subjective nature in it. But today, we have realized those mistakes committed by Watson and his followers and have gone for correcting it by allowing psychology to gain consciousness by accepting metaphysical realities. It was rightly remarked by someone that, in order to become 'natural' science, "psychology lost first its soul and then its mind, and it was left only with the body and behaviour in the hands of behaviourists." This, however, does not mean that we can accept anything in psychology blindly without sufficient evidences. If the concept of reincarnation has been accepted, it is because of the following six convincing evidences researchers have noted (Khoo, 1995).

1. Near Death Experience
2. Out-of-Body Experience
3. Mediumship and Channelling
4. Hypnosis and other Forms of Regression
5. Spontaneous Past-life Recalls
6. Induction by Techniques other than Hypnosis

Volumes of reputed research have been conducted in various fields to support the above mentioned categories of evidences. University professors, scientists, and thinkers like Dr. Ian Stevenson, Dr. T.K. Khoo, Edgar Cayce, Carol Bowman, Gloria Chadwick, Stephen Knapp, Swami Abhedananda, Swami Sivananda and many others have all researched thoroughly into these topics and have accepted reincarnation as a reality. We, therefore, should try to understand the issue on the basis of what they have noted and suggested.

One of the most powerful arguments for upholding the existence of reincarnation is how people are born with different capacities, talents, interests, body defects and birthmarks. How are some children born with inherent talents to be creative, exceptional, and artistic than others? There are many such instances of wonderful powers exhibited by artists and painters when they were quite young. Sankaracharya, the great commentator of the Vedanta philosophy, finished his commentary when he was twelve years old. How could the shepherd Mangiamelo calculate like an arithmetical machine at the age of five? The same is true with another child, Zerah Colburn. When he was under eight years of age, he could solve the most tremendous mathematical problems instantly without using any figures. In one instance, he took the number 8 and raised it up progressively to sixteenth power and instantly mentioned the correct result which contained fifteen figures—281,474,976,710,656. When asked the square root of numbers consisting of six figures, he would state the result instantly with perfect accuracy. He used to give the cube root of numbers in the hundreds of millions the very moment when it was asked. Somebody asked him once how many minutes were there in 48 years, he answered, 25,288,800 (Abhedananda, 2007). The same is true with Shakuntala Devi in India today. All these can be explained only through the doctrine of reincarnation and not by learning.

Some persons may try to explain these instances through heredity. But is it not a fact that the children of the same parents show marked dissimilarities to their parents and to each other? For example, if a man has five children, one is honest and saintly, another is an idiot, the third one is a murderer, the fourth one is a versatile genius, and the fifth one is a crippled and diseased one. Then, how can we say that it is due to heredity? Even the identical twins have dissimilar characters and possess opposite qualities, although they are born of the same parents and brought up under similar conditions and environments. These dissimilarities and body defects, therefore, cannot be explained through heredity. They can be explained only through past-life *karmas* (reincarnation). Moreover, heredity believes in chance factor many times when it fails to explain something, but reincarnation does not believe in chance factor and gives causal explanation for everything.

Is it also not a fact that sometimes we have experienced being here before (Deja Vu) while watching a movie or having a dream or going on a vacation to a new place? Hearing some children saying that they were so and so in their past lives which came to be true to a great extent on verification? Feeling attracted and falling in love with some persons at first sight? All these and many more instances are there to support the existence of reincarnation. Simply saying that such instances are just by chance or merely "divine mysteries" is just avoiding the question or showing ignorance of the divine law.

What is *Karma*?

Karma is a Sanskrit word which literally means '*action*'. But for a human being, action is not just a physical act or behaviour because it also includes his/her intention for doing that behaviour. Intention may be expressed through either physical or verbal actions. According to Tsering (2004), "Intention is the most important of all mental events because it gives direction to the mind, determining whether we engage with virtuous, non-virtuous, or neutral objects. Just as iron is powerlessly drawn to a magnet, our minds are powerlessly drawn to the object of our intentions." Therefore, when we take intention into consideration, we find that the human behaviour becomes "*karma*" because we human beings—not the animals—have the freedom and capacity to judge rightly or wrongly about our behaviour. This freedom gives direction to our mind to choose virtuous, non-virtuous, or neutral objects. This exercise of judgement is known as *karma* for which human life is known as the *karma-bhumi*.

What is Reincarnation?

The word "reincarnation" takes its root from the Latin word, "*in carnis*" which means "in the flesh" or incarnation. In the classic Vedic texts of India, it is called *Samsara* which is a Sanskrit word, and which means being bound to the cycle of repeated birth and death. Therefore, it has been defined as the soul's cyclical return to the earth or other planes until we free ourselves from our negative *karmas* (*Samskaras*) and can be purified and unified permanently into the "ONE" source. It postulates that there is a pre-existing soul before birth and continues after death. According to Khoo (1995), the soul incarnates hundreds or thousands of times to "promote spiritual growth so that the soul can arrive finally at one with the Universe".

"Soul" is a term which is rarely used with precise meaning in philosophy, religion, or common life. It is, however, regarded as descriptive of an entity related to but distinguishable from the body—the spiritual part of human beings that animates their physical existence and survives death. Since every thought and action creates memory and comes back either to bless or haunt us, it creates a field of information around us at the level of energy. We store this information in our mind as we do in a computer. This data or memory is either positive or negative which is also recorded in our soul as a hard disc (Harra, 2002). All the negative memories try to resurface in our life again and again unless they are resolved. As a result, when one dies, his/her soul comes out with such unresolved memories, which are known as his/her *karmas*, and looks for new parents to incarnate (get another body) so that the repairing could be done to what the person did wrong. And this practice continues life after life till all the negative memories are erased from the soul.

How *Karma* and Reincarnation Work

How *karma* works is well expressed in the divine statement: "As you sow, so you reap" like the third law of Newton: "Each action has an equal and opposite reaction." We have seen how the soul travels from one body to the next due to unresolved *karmas*. All these show clearly that we are all governed by the universal "karmic law" and there are no exceptions. Whether we realize it or not, everyday we are creating *karma* with every thought and action. Either we kill an insect, abuse someone, or are jealous of a friend, we are creating bad *karmas*. Similarly, every single positive thing we do, like helping someone, or showing sympathy and love towards someone, creates good *karmas*. In this sense, life is a constant balancing act of offsetting the bad *karmas* with the good ones (Sharan, 2005, 2007). If we don't erase our bad *karmas* or heal them at the end of every day, they accumulate. Such accumulated *karmas*—accumulated over time and sometimes over many life times—work like the "snowball" effect. They go on multiplying and multiplying. We, therefore, need to resolve negative *karmas* everyday either by more and more positive acts or by regular prayer (confession). Otherwise they will never be healed and we have to take birth again and again to live with the consequential sufferings.

How reincarnation works is nicely elaborated in the Vedic texts of India. The *Bhagavad Gita* explains that whatever state of consciousness one attains, when he or she quits this body, a similar state will be attained in the next life. This means that after the person has lived his or her life, the numerous variegated activities of the person form an aggregated consciousness. And when the living beings take birth again, they get a certain kind of body that is most suitable for the type of consciousness they have developed. Therefore, according to *Padma Purana*, there are eighty-four lacs species of life, each offering a particular class of body for whatever kind of desires and consciousness the living being may have in this world. In this sense, the living entity is the son of his past and the father of his future. According to Knapp (2005), "All of our thoughts and actions throughout our life will collectively influence the state of being we are in at the time of death. This consciousness will determine what that person is thinking of at the end of one's life. This last thought and consciousness will then direct where that person will most likely go in the next life because this state of being carries over from this life into the next."

Thus, it is clear that every physical and verbal action is preceded by mental activity. Goodwill motivates a kind gesture; ill will motivates nasty words. The presence of ill will before and during this act has an impact on the mind due to which a certain potential is left behind. This potential is a karmic seed—a seed planted in our mind as well as in the soul (which functions like a hard disc) by physical, verbal or mental action. The strength or depth of this seed is determined by a number of factors; including how strong our intention is, whether we clearly understand what we are doing, whether we act on our intention, and whether the physical and verbal action is completed. Seeds will remain in the soul until they ripen or are destroyed. These seeds are responsible for selecting parents to get an appropriate body in reincarnation. Seeds created by negative mental events and actions, however, can be destroyed by some opponent or antidotal powers. The most important of these powers are regrets for the negative acts and a firm resolution not to act that way again in the future. According to Knapp (2005), "One's state of consciousness or conception of life exists in the subtle body, which consists of mind, intelligence and false ego. The soul is covered by this subtle body, which exists within the gross material form. When the physical vehicles can no longer function, the subtle body and soul are forced out of it. Then, when the time is right, they are placed in another physical frame which properly accommodates the state of mind of the living entity."

This can be explained better by understanding how the seeds of different trees select different materials from the common environment and absorb and assimilate different quantities of elements. Is it not a fact that when two seeds—one of an oak and the other of a chestnut—are planted together in a pot, they germinate and grow differently although the environments, earth, water, heat, etc. are the same? There is some peculiarity in absorbing different quantities of elements and other properties for each seed so that it can maintain its own identity. Similarly, through the law of "natural selection" the subtle body of the dying person chooses and attracts such parts from the common environments which can be helpful in its proper expression or manifestation. Parents are, therefore, nothing but the principal parts of the environment of the re-incarnating individual.

Theory of Transmigration

The theory of transmigration is one of the oldest theories accepted by the people of the Orient to solve the problems concerning life and death as well as to explain the continuity of existence after death. This theory presupposes the existence of the soul as an entity which can live even when the gross material body is dead or dissolved into its elements. The materialists of all ages have refused to accept this theory because they do not admit the existence of the soul. The same is true with many of the scientists because they accept the theory of heredity and endeavour to explain everything by it. But when we examine the arguments cited in favour of heredity, we find that the theory of transmigration is much more satisfactory, much more rational than that of heredity (Abhedananda, 2007). Those who believe in heredity, have to depend on chance factors many times. But those who believe in the theory of transmigration apply the law of *karma* which explains that human souls are bound by this irresistible law and cannot get out of it. Their future birth does not depend upon the chance factor, or upon their whimsical free choice, but upon the thoughts and deeds or misdeeds of their previous lives. According to Swami Abhedananda, "Parents do not create the souls; they have no power to create. They can only give the suitable environments necessary for manufacturing a gross physical body. The souls come with their tendencies, with their desires, and they remain as germs of life." And these germs of life contain vital forces, sense physical and mental powers, and ethereal particles of matter. The Vedanta philosophers also describe these germs as subtle bodies which are subject to evolution and growth. They arise from lower to higher stages of development—from the mineral through the vegetable to the animal kingdom and eventually to human beings. Professor Huxley has rightly said that "None but hasty thinkers will reject it on the ground of inherent absurdity. Like the doctrine of evolution itself, that of transmigration has its roots in the world of reality."

Universal Laws of *Karma* and Reincarnation

Every person should have a comprehensive understanding of the Nature's laws, and their operations. Similarly, he/she should also have a good understanding of the spiritual laws. Then only he or she can pull on well in this world by utilizing the helping forces and neutralizing the hostile or antagonistic currents. All these laws of the Universe are governed by the master law of cause and effect. The cause is, however, invisible in many cases but the effect is visible. The falling of an apple from a tree, for example, is the effect of a certain invisible force called gravitation; suffering of a person is due to his/her past misdeeds. These examples suggest that all visible or perceptible phenomena are but the various expressions of different forces which act as invisible or imperceptible agents upon the subtle and imperceptible forms of matter. These invisible agents or forces together with the imperceptible particles of matter make up the subtle states of the phenomenal Universe. The same explanation is applicable to the law of *karma* and reincarnation. According to Abhedananda (2007), the gross human body is the result of its subtle body which is nothing but a minute germ of a living substance. It contains the invisible particles of matter which are held together by vital force, and it also possesses mind or thought-force in a potential state, just as the seed of a plant contains in it the life force and the power of growth. Every action of body and mind which we do, every thought we have becomes fine, and is stored up in the form of a *Samskara* or impression in our minds. It remains latent for some time, and then rises up in the form of a mental wave and produces new desires known as *Vasanas* or consciousness. According to Vedanta, these *Vasanas* or strong worldly desires are the manufacturers of new bodies. And, if such *Vasanas* or longing for worldly pleasures remain in any subtle body, even after hundreds of births, that person will be born again.

Thus, if *Vasana* (also known as subtle body or consciousness) is understood as basic to everything, it becomes easy to believe in reincarnation because it is governed by certain spiritual laws.

These laws come from and are imbued with Spirit. Therefore, they are also known as Divine Laws. These laws dictate the results of our thoughts and actions. When we perform an action or put our thought, we try to control the results. But we fail to do so because there are too many laws working at too many levels for the ego to manage. This is the reason why the *Bhagavad Gita* says that we should perform our actions consciously with good intentions and leave the results or consequences up to Spirit or Divine Laws.

We have seen that every action or thought has an effect or consequence, and the nature of that effect depends upon the nature of the cause. If the cause is "good", the effect will be good. If the cause comes from negative thoughts or evil, the results will be equally negative or evil. The law of reincarnation is based exactly on this karmic law. We are all energy fixed in time and space based on karmic law. We, therefore, cannot commit *karma* and can expect it to finish with it in one life time. There has to be many lives to resolve one's *karmas*. That means, once *karma* is initiated, it must continue until it is spent. This process of *karma* and reincarnation is based on certain spiritual laws out of which the following three are very important (Khoo, 1995):

1. *Law of Continuation*: We have seen that when the *karma* is initiated, it continues till it is spent fully. We, therefore, need to understand how it continues. Actually, there are three kinds of *karmas*: *Sanchita Karmas*, *Prarabdha Karmas*, and *Kriyaman Karmas*. *Sanchita karma* is the sum total and storehouse of all our actions, good and bad, committed in the innumerable past lives and in the present life. The whole of it is recorded and preserved. *Prarabdha karma* is the ripe *karma* ready to

give its overdue effect in the form of gain and loss in the present life. *Kriyaman karma* is in the course of making it in the future. It is this which preserves our freewill with certain limitations and ensures our success (Sivananda, 2001). Thus, unless all these *karmas* are spent fully, we shall continue to incarnate and re-incarnate.

Sometimes, we face a dilemma. How is that when a person is doing many good things, he or she is getting bad results? The answer is very simple: It is due to his/ her past bad *karmas* (*Prarabdha*). For example, although we are pouring good rice from the top of a grain elevator or silo, we are getting sometimes bad rice from the door at the bottom because it was put earlier. Therefore, once this lot of bad rice is clear, we are bound to get good rice from the same door (Knapp, 2005). The same is true with our *karmas*. Good and bad results are coming because we have good and bad *karmas* stored in our soul.

Law of continuation also has another meaning. It says that some of our good tendencies, traits, habits, talents, and abilities are carried over to the next life. Such characteristics we are strongly associated with tend to be carried over to the next. We find among ourselves persons who are born with some wonderful powers. For example, Shri Ramakrishna was born with God-consciousness, and he went into the highest state of *Samadhi* when he was four years old. Similarly, one person may be born with such a developed power of self-control that others cannot acquire it even after years of hard struggle. Therefore, we have to admit that a few characteristics or qualities are inborn in every person. This, however, does not mean that our all characteristics will be carried over to the next life. Perhaps, it is only those characteristics which are very good and we are strongly associated with them particularly at the time of death.

2. *Law of Consequence:* The law of consequence, which is also known as the law of rebirth, is the most fundamental law in human destiny. This is, however, not a static law. We constantly use it to create new destiny to improve the old destiny brought from the past. We all have lived many lives on this earth in the past and shall be living many more in the future. In each of these past lives, we have gone for good and bad *karmas* which have attracted good and bad reactions affecting our consciousness. This consciousness, consisting of thinking, feeling, and willing, has covered the soul with a subtle body made up of mind, intelligence and false ego. The shape of the subtle body is said to change according to the type of consciousness we develop. This subtle body travels with the soul from one material body to another, or even in between material bodies, as we go through the rounds of repeated birth and death. It is thus the consciousness, which we develop during our life time, is responsible for our rebirths and new bodies. This is the reason why the law of consequence is known as companion to the law of rebirth.

It has been rightly described in the "Western Wisdom Teachings" that there is an invisible institution in every person which is functioning like a Universal Bank where we make a deposit of every good thought, feeling, and action. "All our constructive work, our self-discipline, our service to others, and all our other actions which are in harmony with the Divine Will make deposits in the Universal Bank. These deposits are the source from which we draw our destiny, our good fortune, and our opportunities. The unseen Director of this Bank, together with the Agents of Destiny, keeps an unerring record of all deposits." And, from time to time, the Director declares a dividend in the form of some opportunity, success, good luck, or "wind-fall". Since the Universal Bank is backed by the Universe, it cannot fail. We can never lose nor can we get more than what we deserve. If our destiny and success are not what we would like them to be, then it is because our credit in the Universal Bank has been temporarily depleted. In such a case, there is nothing to do but get busy to make new deposits. If we wish to change our environment and fortune, we should change our thought patterns by developing *'creative power of thought'*. Since two thoughts cannot occupy the mind at the same time, we simply need to replace destructive thoughts by constructive thoughts. The negative desires like anger, hate, revenge, resentment, etc. disrupt and disarrange creative power of thought. We, therefore, need to substitute them by positive desires like love, respect, trust, and kind attitude.

3. *Law of Compensation:* As we progress in our life, we are bound to experience innumerable facets of life. In some lives we have to be physically strong and in some week; in some we have to be intellectually active and in others mentally subdued. Not only that, we also need to change our sex, race and religion to round up our education. All these are due to law of compensation which operates everywhere in Nature's phenomena.

According to Swami Sivananda, the law of compensation also refers to the perfect balance between the cause and effect. The seed breaks and then only a big tree comes out of it. Water becomes steam and the steam moves the engine. Similarly, when the sulphuric acid in a jar of a battery is consumed, electricity is produced in a bulb to give light. We find that this law of compensation is operating everywhere in the Nature. It is for this reason the *Bhagavad Gita* says that "Birth must be followed by death and death must be followed by birth." Vedanta also maintains that "Nothing is destroyed in the Universe." Today scientists are also supporting this view that "non-existence can never become existence and existence can never become non-existence." Based on this principle, we can say that the impressions or consciousness which we have now will never be destroyed and will remain with us in one form or the other. Therefore, even if our bodies die, the *karmas* or *Samskaras* remain in our souls in the form of a subtle body. And that subtle body of the soul gets another body sooner or later.

Conclusion

In order to understand reincarnation, first we have to realize that we are not only the bodies, but we also have minds and souls within us. Mind is an internal instrument functioning like a mirror on which the soul is throwing lights constantly. Thereby, the mind is getting the power of consciousness only from the soul (Sharan, 2007). According to the *Srimad-Bhagavatam*, the soul is self-luminous, beyond birth and death, and unlimited by time and space and, therefore, beyond all change. As one witnesses the birth and death of a tree, similarly, the soul experiences the birth, death, and various activities of the body like a separate entity in it. In this process, under the influence of *karma* (*Vasana*), the soul is covered by a subtle body which becomes capable of manufacturing another material body according to its desires and tendencies. Just as a germ of life develops a grosser form by cellular sub-division by growth and by assimilation of the environmental conditions, so the germ of the human soul manufactures the body by obeying the laws which govern the physical plane. Parents are thus nothing but the channels through which the migrating souls receive their material forms. Parents do not create the souls because they do not have powers to create. However, they provide suitable environment necessary for manufacturing a gross physical body. It is not possible for anyone to see what type of subtle body or consciousness is being carried over by the soul at the time of death. But every soul, covered by the subtle body, has to look for another materialistic body to take up where it left off in the previous existence. Knapp (2005) has rightly said that "... the next life may be in another physical body or in a subtle body in between births, or even in heavenly or hellish states of being."

The phenomena of the Universe, as reported by science, are subject to evolution—a gradual change and progressive development from a relatively uniform condition to relative complexity. From the greatest solar system down to the smallest blade of grass, everything in the Universe has taken its present shape and form through this cosmic process of evolution. The sun, moon, stars, satellites and other planets have come into existence by going through innumerable changes produced by the evolutionary process of the cosmos. The same is true with reincarnation. Embryology—a branch of life science—has also proved that "man is the epitome of the whole creation." It tells that the human body before its birth passes through all the different stages of the animal kingdom—such as the polyp, fish, reptile, dog, ape, and at last, man (Abhedananda, 2007).

The process of evolution, as science says, is governed by three laws: Tendency to vary, natural selection, and struggle for existence. With the same laws, science also tries to explain the physical, mental, and spiritual evolution of mankind. So far the first two (physical and mental) evolutions are concerned, yes; the science seems to be correct. But what about the spiritual evolution? It is a fact that every human being has animal nature. Therefore, Darwin seems to be right when he says that human beings are just the developed form of lower animals. But his evolution theory fails to explain how every human being is also spiritual in nature. Since no animal has morality or spirituality as such, it cannot be expected that this kind of nature has evolved from animals in human beings. This is, therefore, not a case of evolution but of a creation or sudden development.

Actually, as Vedanta says, each germ of life possesses infinite potentialities and infinite possibilities. It contains vital forces, sense powers, psychic powers, and ethereal particles of matter. At the time of death, the soul contracts and withdraws all its powers from the sense organs to its innermost centre, and in that contracted state it leaves the body like a seed. By the law of persistence of force and conservation of energy, these powers remain latent in that centre until environmental conditions become favourable for their manifestations. Rebirth gives a chance for their manifestations. However, their manifestations are controlled by limitations of each material body the soul chooses.

We have seen above that the process of reincarnation starts from the mineral through the vegetable to the animal kingdom and finally, to the human beings. The reason is that the soul wants to have all sorts of experiences so that finally it gets a human body and thereby it gets a chance to liberate itself. In human body, all powers of the contracted soul get a chance to manifest themselves fully which was not possible in any other body. This is the reason why the human body is said to be a perfect body for the incarnating soul.

There is another advantage of the human body. The spiritual power of the soul also gets manifested in this body which was not possible in any other body. With the help of this spiritual power, a person can be completely free from all the worldly desires. He/she can be engaged only in good *karmas* as a selfless person without being 'involved' in them. Not only that, even if something wrong is committed, it will be resolved by him or her at the earliest either through confession or through regular prayer. As a result of that, when he or she will die, there will not be any debt for the soul to pay back. And, once the soul is free from any such debt, it will not be covered by any subtle body (*Vasana*). This way, it will get liberated and will merge with God.

References

Abhedananda, Swami. (2007). *Reincarnation*. www. booksboost. com

Chadwick, G. (1988). *Discovering your past lives*. Illinois: Contemporary Books.

Harra, C. (2002). *Everyday karma*. New York: Ballantine Books.

Khoo, T.K. (1995). *Universal law of reincarnation*. khengkoo_t@hotmail.com

Knapp, S.M. (2005). *Reincarnation and karma: How they really affect us*. www.iuniverse.com

Sharan, M.B. (2005). Vedantic approach to the understanding of human mind, behaviour, and karma. *Indian Journal of Community Psychology*, 1, 1-9.

Sharan, M.B. (2007). Making psychology complete and essential for understanding of the human mind, behaviour and intuitive awareness. *Psychological Studies*, 62 (3), 187-195.

Sivananda, Swami. (1995). *Practice of karma yoga* (4th Ed.). Uttaranchal: A Divine Life Society Publication.

Stevenson, I. (1974). *Twenty cases suggestive of reincarnation* (2nd Ed.). Virginia: The University Press of Virginia.

Tsering, G.T. (2004). *The Buddha's medicine for the mind* (24th Impression). Kolkata: Advaita Ashrama.

Yogananda, Paramhansa. (2007). *Karma and reincarnation: The wisdom of Yogananda*. CA: Crystal Clarity Publishers.

6

Law of Interpersonal Attraction and the Soulmate Relationships

Law of Interpersonal Attraction

Interpersonal attraction is the attraction between people which leads to acquaintances, friendships and intimate relationships. It can be viewed as a force acting between two people that tends to draw them together, connect them, and resist their separation. It is a relatively long-term relationship between two or more people based on emotions like love and liking, regular business interactions, or some other type of social commitment. It takes place in a great variety of contexts, such as family, friends, marriage, work, clubs, neighbourhoods, and societies. They may be regulated by law, custom, or mutual agreements, and are the basis of social groups and society as a whole. All relationships involve some level of interdependence and, therefore, people in a relationship tend to influence each other, share their thoughts and feelings, and engage in activities together.

Scientific Explanation

Many factors leading to interpersonal attraction have been studied by psychologists, sociologists, anthropologists and social workers. The most frequently studied factors are: physical attractiveness, propinquity, similarity, complementarity, reciprocal liking and reinforcement.

Physical Attractiveness: It is said that love and justice are blind. Many studies, however, do find a relationship between appearance and at least the initial level of attraction. This is because physical appearance is relatively easy to quantify and is one of the most visible characteristics that enter into choosing a partner. Some studies suggest that people are more likely to form long standing relationships with those who are equally physically attractive as they are. Miller and Brehm (2006), for example, found that the probability of acceptance is high in the case of physically attractive persons. According to Murstein (1971), when photos of dating and engaged couples were rated in terms of attractiveness, a definite tendency was found for couples of similar attractiveness to date and engage. The concept of beauty, however, varies from culture to culture. But "there is a fairly universal agreement that the physical appearance of a woman is more central to their overall attractiveness than it is for men" (Wilson and Niyas, 1976).

Propinquity: According to Miller and Brehm (2006), the propinquity effect can be defined as: "the more we see and interact with a person, the more likely he or she is to become our friend or intimate partner." This has been rightly said that both friendships and intimate relationships are most likely to develop between persons who frequently cross each other's paths. This effect is very similar to the mere exposure in that the more a person is exposed to a stimulus, the more he likes it. However, there are a few exceptions to the mere exposure effect.

The social allergy effect occurs when a person's annoying habits grow worse over time.

Similarity: "Birds of a feather flock together" points out that similarity is a crucial determinant of interpersonal attraction. According to Morry's attraction-similarity model (2007), there is a lay belief that people with actual similarity produce initial attraction. Perceived similarity develops for someone to rate others as similar to themselves in on-going relationship. Such perception is either self-serving (friendship) or relationship-serving (romantic relationship). Newcomb (1963) also points out that people tend to change perceived similarity to obtain balance in a relationship. Additionally, perceived similarity has been found to be greater than actual similarity in predicting interpersonal attraction. Findings also suggest that interpersonal similarity and attraction are multidimensional constructs (Lydon, Jamieson the Zanna, 1988) in which people are attracted to others who are similar to them in demographics, physical appearance, attitudes, interpersonal style, social and cultural background, personality, interests and activities preferences, and communication and social skills.

Complementarity: Some studies suggest that the "opposites attract." Complementary partners prefer closer interpersonal relationship than non-complementary ones (Nowicki & Manheim, 1991). Couples who reported the highest level of loving and harmonious relationship were more dissimilar in dominance than couples who scored lower in relationship quality (Markey & Markey, 2007). We are attracted to people who complement to us because this allows us to have more and more satisfying interactions and maintain our preferred style of behaviour. Winch and his associates (1955) argue that when the needs of two people combine in a complementary fashion, attraction results.

Reciprocal Liking and Reinforcement: No one likes to be rejected. Therefore, we are usually not attracted to others unless the feeling seems reciprocal or two-way. According to Berscheid and Walster (1978), reciprocity rule seems to be the strongest rule of attraction in human relationships. Social exchange theory (Homans, 1961) interprets relationships in terms of exchanged benefits. According to this theory, the decision to begin or continue a relationship depends on the same kinds of factors that operate in economic marketplace: rewards, costs, and available alternatives. It predicts that people regard relationships in terms of rewards obtained from the relationship, as well as the potential rewards from alternate relationships. Rewards make relationship worthwhile and enjoyable whereas costs cause irritation. Therefore, in a relationship, if the obtained rewards are lower and the costs are higher, both the parties may become dissatisfied and unhappy. However, people's expectations of rewards or costs depend on the time invested in the relationship.

To sum up, it can be said that interpersonal relationships are dynamic systems that change continuously during their existence. Like living organisms, relationships have a beginning, a lifespan, and an end. They tend to grow and improve gradually, as people get to know each other, try to have more and more satisfying interactions, and become closer emotionally. One of the most influential models of relationship development has been proposed by Levinger (1983) which is formulated to describe heterosexual, adult romantic relationships, but is applicable to other kinds of relationships as well. According to this model, the natural development of a relationship follows five stages:

1. *Acquaintance:* Becoming acquainted depends on several factors—physical proximity, similarity, first impressions, and a variety of other factors.

2. *Buildup:* During this stage, people begin to trust and care about each other. The need for compatibility and such filtering agents as common background and goals will decide whether or not interaction continues.
3. *Continuation:* This stage follows a mutual commitment to a long-term friendship, romantic relationship, or marriage. It is generally a long and stable period in which continued growth and development will occur. Mutual trust is important for sustaining the relationship.
4. *Deterioration:* Not all relationships deteriorate, but those that do tend to show signs of trouble. Boredom, resentment, and dissatisfaction may occur, and partners may communicate less and avoid self-disclosure. Loss of trust and betrayals may take place as the downward spiral continues.
5. *Termination:* The final stage marks the end of the relationship, either by death in the case of a healthy relationship, or by separation.

Spiritual Explanation

Our life is governed not only by the physical laws like laws of electricity, chemistry, hydraulics, atomic physics, and so on but also by the spiritual laws like laws of ***karma***, increase (or decrease), balance, wisdom, attraction and so on. Such spiritual laws like physical laws are universal in nature and are understandable, unchangeable, and inevitable. We, therefore, need to recognize these spiritual laws which are also known as laws of consciousness or laws of mind and spirit.

Many persons believe that the *Law of Attraction* works by aligning God or the Universe with our wishes. We are all made of energy, and our energy operates at different frequencies. We can change our frequency of energy with ***positive thoughts***, especially by expressing gratitude to God for what He has given to us. According to Scott (2008), "By using grateful, positive thoughts and feelings and by focusing on our dreams (rather than our frustrations), we can change the frequency of our energy, and the law of attraction brings positive things (things of that frequency) into our lives. What we attract depends on where and how we focus our attention, but we must believe that it's already ours, or soon will be."

It is a fact that the physical Universe is composed of energy, and ultimately, of thought because energy and mass are convertible. Since each pattern of energy has a unique frequency or vibration, each thought pattern also has a unique frequency or vibration. Emotions are strong vibrational energy patterns. Therefore, powerful emotion—positive or negative—is bound to draw the thought(s) behind them more quickly into the real life experience. Positive thoughts generate positive emotion and draw positive life experience; negative thoughts generate negative emotion and draw negative life experience. This is the reason why the law of attraction works by using grateful positive thoughts and feelings. "It is the law that determines the complete order in the Universe, every moment of your life, and every single thing you experience in your life. It doesn't matter who you are or where you are, the law of attraction is forming your entire life experience, and this all-powerful law is doing that through your thoughts. You are the one who calls the law of attraction into action, and you do it through your thoughts" (Byrne, 2006).

How to Get a Soul Mate?

The term "soul mate" has been used by different authors in different ways. Recently, the concept of meeting our soul mate has become so popular that there are hundreds, if not thousands, of books and articles to suggest how to attract One into our life. They say that there are souls we have experienced with in our past lives or are experiencing at this time in different bodies, and with whom, we have a feeling of deep and natural affinity, friendship, love, intimacy, sexuality, and/or compatibility. Soul mates can have various types of relationships, which do not always include romantic love or sex. They can be close friends, co-workers, teachers, or others who have influenced our life in one way or the other. They play the emotional, spiritual, physical, and mental games with us and are affecting our relationships in a positive or negative way. For some persons, a soul-mate relationship is one in which there are no challenges, no conflicts, no strife, only the opportunity to explore one another as equals, sharing joys, consoling sorrows, and being indivisible when united as one. For others, however, such a relationship is not so much as an immediate reality but rather as a goal towards which they can grow. Regardless of whether it is seen as something created or something destined from birth, most individuals perceive a soul-mate relationship as being preferable to "just a relationship".

Some persons are of the opinion that the term "soul mate" cannot be used in plural form (soul mates) because everyone has only one soul mate. And this soul mate is the other half of that person (male or female) waiting for reunion and reconnection in the present like twin flame. Twin flame is supposed to be someone with whom one has spent lifetime after lifetime in the past with an endless exchange of love, romance, and relationships and is eager to have the same in the present. Perhaps, this is the reason why it is said that "marriages are arranged in the heaven but performed on the earth." It is also believed that when one meets such person, he or she is able to recognize that person with just one look and falls in love at first sight. Something like sparks fly, and there is an instantaneous and unexplainable chemistry between the two. And once they come together, they live together life-long with perfect and unending love, and promise to remain together again in their next lives.

It is true that no scientific evidence can be given to prove the concept of soul mates or twin flames. However, this can be accepted as a metaphysical reality. When we believe in the universal laws of *karma* and reincarnation (Sharan, 2009) and interrelate ourselves on subtle levels *via* our actions, thoughts, feelings and emotions, how can we deny the existence of soul mates or twin flames or twin souls? Perhaps, this is the reason why this concept has acquired a lot of attention recently, especially with the advent of the movies like *The Secret* in Western countries which supports strongly the Law of Attraction. Based on all these, it can be inferred safely that if one thinks and does the right things, and has the right feelings, his/her ideal mate is bound to appear magically one day as a soul mate. Since twin flames are eager to meet with each other, they find out their ways. And we know, for souls, time and space is not a problem at all. Moreover, the theory of reincarnation says that when souls choose to enter into physicality, they are split into masculine and feminine aspects. As a result, when they take birth and grow to become youngsters, they want to meet anyhow to unite.

In practice, however, the likelihood of finding a genuine soul mate totally by chance is rare. One can consider himself/herself very lucky when it happens. Therefore, one has to get ready to find out his/her soul mate. According to Springett (2008), the greatest power to attract the desired soul mate is the will-power of the interested person. If one can muster all his/her will-power and put it behind the aims that he/she finds worthwhile, he/she is bound to get what he/she wants including the love of his/her life. She has suggested the following exercise as a part of the wish-practice method which can be used to attract the soul mate or anything one wants in his/her life:

- Get comfortable and allow yourself to dream clearly about your desired soul mate. Visualize it in all aspects that are really important for you.
- If you find yourself dreaming about a person you know, or someone famous, be clear whether you want that person or you are using him or her as a model. See or feel this person in your mind without being too specific about his/her wealth and hair colour; instead try to sense his/her character and inner qualities.
- Finish this exercise when you feel that you have got that wonderful person. Remember, you will never get a 'perfect' match, and, therefore, you have to go for a compromise on a few aspects.

Note: Keep up your wish for your soul mate at all times without getting impatient or pushy. And practice this inner communication as often and as long as you like. This exercise will create and strengthen the spiritual connection with the person you are looking for.

Male and Female Energy

In a soul-mate relationship, this kind of realization is a must that both the partners need each other to be 'complete'. Since one is a male and the other is a female, their energies need to be merged with each other to create the sense of completeness. It is just not possible to experience the real romantic and erotic passion without the expression of feminine energy as a woman and masculine energy as a man. These two opposites, therefore, need each other in order to ignite romance and sexual feelings as wood needs oxygen to ignite a fire. It is thus the very incompleteness in ourselves that creates the wish in us to unite with the other lovingly on all levels—sexually, emotionally, mentally and spiritually. Perhaps, this is the reason why soul mates are also known as twin flames. Springett (2008) has rightly said that the best way to think of femininity and masculinity is to see them as talents or as natural inclinations. The trouble starts when we are not allowed to express our natural inclinations for one reason or the other. In a soulmate relationship we should always feel safe and comfortable sharing the deepest parts of ourselves. There should be a good give and take of energy and ideas and it should be honest, passionate and healthy. Along with this, the soul mates should accept each other as they are.

The term "soul mate" however, cannot be used only for husband and wife. In real sense, a soul mate is someone we are close to at soul level, and with whom we have had many shared experiences in different lifetimes in various kinds of relationships—sibling, parent-child, teacher-student, best friend, as well as romantic relationships. There is a deep love for each other, and a spiritual bond that sets them apart from other people in our life. Sometimes, this kind of love can be also for pet animals and birds. We have thus many soul mates in our lives, and they come to us to help us grow spiritually. The job of our soul mates is to reflect back to us areas in our lives that are in need of healing. With our soul mates, we can work together to get to the bottom of a conflict, discover our hidden motivations or uncover deeply held fears that keep us reacting in negative ways. They are aware of each others' thoughts, feelings, desires and needs at a level that is hard to imagine. The depth of LOVE is such that they are ONE.

Creating Soul-Mate Relationships

A human relationship is a *living* system like an *organism* which has the tendency to grow. "We want you to think of your union with your partner as a vital living *organism*. It's a new being which the two of you have created, and it's alive! It can continue to live and grow and to contribute much to your individual lives and fulfilment if you nurture it and treat it like the valuable resource it can become for you and for your love partner" (Emmons & Alberti, 1991). In a soulmate relationship, all persons have to learn about *Accepting Each Other* and how to enhance the *Intimacy* in their loving partnership: "If love is the *feeling* that makes the world go *'round'*, intimacy is the ointment that greases the axle." Emmons and Alberti have come up with six key dimensions, which they believe provide a comprehensive framework for viewing and enhancing relationships. All these six dimensions have been presented as "The ACCEPT Model of Relationships" which says that the quality of intimacy or acceptance is determined by these characteristics: mutual *attraction* (A), open and honest *communication* (C), *commitment* to the continuation of the partnership (C), *enjoyment* of their life together (E), a sense of *purpose* for this relationship (P), and a mutual *trust* which honours and respects the other (T). All these factors are equally important and one has to simply maintain a balance among these factors. With this kind of balance, any person can get more and more from this relationship provided he/she has the art of developing it carefully.

For the first half of the twentieth century, individuals from all walks of life and religious backgrounds came to Edgar Cayce and received advice for improving their relationships with spouses, friends, families, work associates, and even with enemies. In all cases, Cayce outlined the same principles that "creating soul mate relationships with every individual in our life is one of our purposes for being in the earth" (Todeschi, 2007). Over the years, in seeking advices for their various problems, individuals have found a number of premises contained in the information of Edgar Cayce:

- Ultimately, all relationships have the potential to be a purposeful and a helpful experience in terms of soul growth and personal transformation.
- We learn most about ourselves through our interactions with others.
- Our relationships with one another are destined to be repeated until they are healed.
- As souls seeking personal wholeness, our goal is to eventually create soul-mate relationships with every individual in our lives.

According to Springett (2008), "A true soul-mate relationship is like an exquisitely beautiful flower that only grows in a well-cared-for and protected place. This flower has a wonderfully delicate scent that will enchant anyone who comes near. The joy and happiness of two people who are entwined in a true soulmate relationship can radiate far beyond the boundaries of their personal communion, and reach the hearts and minds of those who are longing for hope and truth." She adds further that anyone can cultivate this special flower in his/her own garden. For this, he/she needs to learn from where to get the seeds, and how to plant, nourish and protect the plant. She guarantees that if the following four dynamics are properly understood and carefully put into practice, a soul-mate relationship can be achieved:

Commitment to Love and to Grow in Love: It is the deep commitment of both the partners to love and grow in love that makes an ordinary relationship into a soul-mate relationship. For this, they need to learn about how to take care of each other and how to sort out differences, if any. Edgar Cayce has also said the same thing that the soul-mate relationship is an ongoing connection with another individual and that connection enables both the individuals to come to know themselves and to grow in their awareness of their relationship with the Creator.

The Law of an Even Deal: In Buddhism, this law is called '***karma***' which means you get back what you give out or 'as you sow so shall you reap.' If we look at relationship from this viewpoint, we shall come to understand that couples tend to match each other as keys match their keyholes. The two main areas in which partners match are:

- They consciously or unconsciously share some important values and interests, which indicates their level of maturity.
- They match in the even deal they have built around these values.

Harmonious and Erotic Patterns Between Female and Male Energies: Both the feminine and masculine energies blossom most beautifully if they are balanced to a smaller degree by their complementary energies. If men are *too* masculine, they can become ruthless and overbearing, and may start brcaking moral and legal rules in order to achieve their aims. Similarly, if women are *too* feminine, they find it very difficult to get up and do anything in order to change things for the better. Thus, soul-mate relationships can be made heaven for women and paradise for men only when both the energies are valued and desired in the most beautiful way.

The Unavoidable Merging Process Between two People: People who are in love clearly take feelings, attitudes, and even bodily sensations from each other. In fact, the energy fields of two people in a sexual and loving relationship merge more and more into one energy field that envelopes both people and allows both of them to draw on a much greater variety of feelings, ideas and responses to the world. Therefore, in a long-term relationship, both the partners can exchange so much energy with each other that they become literally more and more alike. The woman, for example, can become genuinely stronger and more dominant without losing her soft and tender femininity, and the man can become genuinely softer and more caring without losing his masculine strength. This way, both the partners can enrich their own personalities in a very positive and healthy way, and can maintain soul-mate relationship lifelong.

Conclusion

We have seen how our need for people can make us dependent upon others. However, we have to learn how to enjoy the give-and-take of human relationships while remaining true to our own needs. Social psychologists have discovered several factors that help determine which relationships blossom and which ones get nipped in the bud. In general, they find that people are drawn to those who are (1) geographically available; (2) socially "appropriate"; (3) physically appealing; (4) similar or complementary to themselves; and (5) likely to respond in kind. But, apart from these scientific explanations, there are some spiritual explanations as well. They assume that there are souls we have experienced within our past lives, and are experiencing again with them at this time in different bodies. And, every time, we have had a feeling of deep and natural affinity, friendship, love, intimacy, sexuality, and/or compatibility with them. Such persons are known as soul mates because the attractions are at the soul level. These attractions are sometimes instant (love at first sight) but many times by natural choice. And once they come together, they live together lifelong with perfect and unending love, and promise to remain together again in their next lives.

A human relationship is dynamic in nature. Like a living organism, it goes on changing and growing. While ordinary relationships aim to be static and stable, soul-mate relationships develop and grow like a beautiful flower. This, however, does not happen suddenly or by chance; we have to rather work for it. We have to nurture it and treat it like a valuable resource. It has been rightly said by Springett (2008) that "A soul-mate relationship is actually a means of bringing out the best in us and making us more complete and whole over time than we have been before." As summarized by Diamond in *The Secret* (Byrne, 2006), followings are the secrets to relationships:

- When you want to attract a relationship, make sure your thoughts, works, actions, and surroundings don't contradict your desires.
- Your job is you. Unless you fill yourself up first, you have nothing to give anybody.
- Teat yourself with love and respect, and you will attract people who show you love and respect.
- When you feel bad about yourself, you block the love and instead you attract more people and situations that will continue to make you feel bad about you.
- Focus on the qualities you love about yourself and the law of attraction will show you more great things about you.
- To make a relationship work, focus on what you appreciate about the other person, and not your complaints. When you focus on the strengths, you will get more of them.

While following these secrets, however, we should not forget that the ultimate aim of creating soulmate relationships is to become whole so that finally we are connected to the Creator.

References

Berscheid, E., & Walster, E.H. (1978). *Interpersonal Attraction.* MA: Addison-Wesley.

Byrne, R. (2006). *The Secret.* NY: Beyond Words.

Emmons, M.L., & Alberti, R.E. (1991). *Accepting Each Other.* CA: Impact Publishers.

Homans, G.C. (1961). *Social Behaviour: Its Elementary Forms.* NY: Harcourt, Brace & World.

Levinger, G. (1983). Development and change. In H.H. Kelley, *et al.* (Eds.), *Close Relationships.* (pp. 315-359). NY: W.H. Freeman & Company.

Lydon, J.E., Jamieson, D.W., & Zanna, M.P. (1988). Interpersonal similarity and the social and intellectual dimensions of first impressions. *Social Cognition*, *6*, 269-286.

Markey, P.M., & Markey, C.N. (2007). Romantic ideals, romantic obtainment, and relationship experiences: The complementarity of interpersonal traits among romantic partners. *Journal of Social and Personal Relationships*, *24*, 517-533.

Miller, R.P., & Brehm, S. (2006). *Intimate Relationships.* NY: McGraw-Hill.

Morry, M.M. (2007). Relationship satisfaction as a predictor of perceived similarity among cross-sex friends: A test of the attraction-similarity model. *Journal of Social and Personal Relationship*, *24*, 117-138.

Murstein, B.I. (1971). A theory of marital choice and its applicability to marriage adjustment and friendship. In B.I. Murstein (Ed), *Theories of Attraction and Love*. NY: Springer.

Newcomb, T.M. (1963). Stabilities underlying changes in interpersonal attraction. *Journal of Abnormal and Social Psychology*, *66*, 376-386.

Nowicki, S., Jr., & Manheim, S. (1991). Interpersonal complementarity and time of interaction in female relationships. *Journal of Research in Personality, 25*, 322-333.

Scott, E. (2008). Understanding and using the law of attraction in your life. About.com.

Sharan, M.B. (2009). Universal laws of karma and reincarnation. *The Intuitive-Connections Network*, May, 2009.

Springett, U. (2008). *Soul-mate Relationships*. NY: Harper Collins Publishers.

Todeschi, J.K. (2007). Edgar Cayce on Soul Mates. VA: A.R.E. Press.

Wilson, G., & Niyas, D. (1976). *Love's Mysteries: The psychology of Sexual Attraction*. London: Open Books.

Winch, R.F., Ktsanes, T., & Ktsanes, V. (1955). Empirical elaboration of the theory of complementary needs in mate selection. *Journal of Abnormal and Social Psychology, 51*, 508-513.

7

Our Life: Why is It the Way It is?

(Special Lecture delivered at 14th Annual Conference of the National Academy of Psychology held at IIT, Kharagpur from February 26 to 28, 2004)

In the last few decades, there has been a rapid advancement in the study of genetics and molecular biology, which has provided us additional insights into the questions of life and evolutions. Scientists have unravelled many mysteries behind various life processes, structures and functions of biomolecules. Through chemical analysis, they have found that the bodies of living organisms are primarily made up of four elements—H, O, N and C. Chemicals such as water, proteins, lipids, carbohydrates and nucleic acids constitute 95 per cent of all the molecules present in the body while minerals constitute about 4 per cent of a living organism (Power, 1997). Thus they have felt tempted to conclude that life could be a product of complex chemical reactions. But two Nobel laureates in Biology, Professor Wald and Professor Arber, who have examined this possibility extensively, have concluded recently that "life is possibly beyond molecules" (Singh, 2004). It would be, therefore, worthwhile to examine alternative paradigms of life.

According to Vedanta, the ancient spiritual science of India, all living beings are animated by presence of a non-chemical or non-molecular fundamental spiritual particle called *atman* which has the following characteristics (Singh, 2005):

1. It is the spiritual energy as opposed to the material energy of God,
2. It is a transcendental particle and is ontologically different from matter,
3. It is only due to the interaction between the *atman* and material elements that the material body appears to be active and lively,
4. Its fundamental qualities are: (a) consciousness, (b) free will, (c) intentions, and (d) purpose,
5. It is beyond ordinary sense perceptions but it can be inferred. Consciousness is the most visible symptom of life, *atman*. Matter, however complex it may be, can never be conscious,
6. It exists eternally and it cannot be created or destroyed,
7. It has a will to acquire knowledge,
8. It has a will to be blissful,
9. It has attractive power not only with individual beings but also with matter.

Vedanta described further that only due to the presence of *atman*, the body is animated and active, and undergoes six types of transformation: it takes birth, it lives for sometime, it grows, it produces offspring, it gradually dwindles, and, at last, vanishes into oblivion. When someone dies, one can experience the symptoms of the passing of the *atman* through the eyes, mouth, rectum, or through the head.

Life and Consciousness

Nobody can deny that consciousness is one of the most important characteristics of life which is fundamental of the *atman*. All living beings—microorganisms, birds, animals, etc.—possess different degrees of consciousness. Microorganisms exhibit very little symptom of consciousness because of very thick layers of covering of the material modes. But, they possess consciousness. Well-known Biologists like George Wald and Lynn Marguilies have also indicated that Protozoa, single-celled animals and bacteria also possess consciousness. In other words, these living beings are covered by different degrees of the three modes of material nature—*sattvam* (goodness), *rajah* (passion) and *tamah* (ignorance). The living entities behave differently when they interact with these modes. The mode of goodness is purer than the other two modes and all living beings are influenced to different degrees by the different modes of the nature.

Any activity that the living entity performs is called *karma*. It is a Sanskrit word which means action—physical and psychological—performed by the living entity under the influence of the three modes of material nature (*gunas*). All living beings are engaged in different activities. These activities are being carried out from time immemorial and the living entities are enjoying or suffering the fruits of these called the law of *karma*. In Vedantic tradition, the law of *karma* states that every living entity has a predestined happiness and distress in his/her present body according to the actions performed by the living entity in his/her previous and present life. The concept of *karma* is similar to that of action and reaction in Newton's Law.

Spiritual Evolution and Uniqueness of Human Life

Vedantic science describes evolution as the journey of the innumerable conscious particles of life in time and space as they travel from one form of body to another under the law of *karma* (cause and effect). Each living entity's degree or level of consciousness, *guna* and *karma* will determine the direction of his/her evolutionary path. Darwin's mistake was that he could not conceive the existence of consciousness or a spiritual soul. Thus, Vedanta does not accept Darwin's theory of evolution. Under normal circumstances, consciousness evolves linearly as well as step-wise. The different bodies or forms to accommodate a specific conscious being are already arranged by nature within a cosmic plan: there are 8,400,000 forms of life and one gets the human form of life after having changed 8.4×10^6 other forms of life (Singh, 2005).

The quest for understanding the deeper meaning of life is the turning point in the life of individuals. Since the conscious intelligence is fully developed in the case of human beings, only they can make different levels of inquiry including the Absolute Truth. This ability to inquire about the ultimate truth of life makes the human being uniquely different from all other forms of life. A bird can ask itself—where is water?, where is food?, but not ponder the meaning of its existence. Similarly, a frog cannot have vision; it can simply react to light like a photo electrically activated garage door (Wald, 2004). A computer that has just beaten a human player at chess cannot feel elevated. Thus, Vedanta emphasizes that the primary subject matter of the human form of life is to inquire about the science of Absolute Truth God.

In the human form of life, consciousness (*cetana*), intelligence (*buddhi*), mind (*manas*), senses (*indriyas)* are fully developed. Therefore, a human being is totally equipped to make the deepest inquiry (*jijnasa*)—the spiritual inquiry. A similar message echoes in the statement of Albert Einstein who states that "knowing the plan of God is most important and the rest are details. By this inquiry, *sambandha*, the relationship between the self and God will be established and the pure spiritual knowledge of the self will be understood" (Singh, 2005).

Is Our Life Regulated by Certain Universal Laws?

We are all aware of many, many physical laws—laws of electricity, chemistry, hydraulics, atomic physics, radio transmission, etc. When night falls, all of us see the stars and planets in their stately movement by the law of planetary motion. When we switch on light, the room gets illuminated as the laws of electricity operate precisely and predictably. That means, in the Universe, everything—cars, telephones, television sets, etc.—operates in accordance with certain universal physical laws. Similarly, our life is also affected by certain laws of mind and spirit. Many sources, ancient and modern, including all religious books and other sacred texts, assure us that there are many such universal laws which interact in our lives. Like physical laws, these spiritual laws are also universal in nature and are unbreakable, unchangeable, and inevitable. "It would not have been logical or consistent for the Creator to provide precise laws for the physical world and have left the functioning of the mental/spiritual world of human kind to chance or worse" (McArthur, 1993). We, therefore, simply need to recognize these spiritual laws which are also known as laws of consciousness or laws of mind action. By knowing these laws and employing them effectively, we can change our lives dramatically.

Even a swimmer knows that the law of gravity will cause him/her to sink. But, through the application of law of floatation by using a float of some sort, he or she can swim successfully. Similarly, all of the spiritual laws give us the basic principles involved in guiding our lives for transformation.

These laws provide a clear path to follow by which we can progress and make our lives and our world what we would like it to be. According to McArthur (1993), "The great joy, the great hope, the answer to this paradox lies in coming to an understanding of the Universal Laws, for they create both conditions. They create chaos and suffering when we misapply them. They create beauty and harmony in our lives when we use them in the highest way."

What are the Universal Spiritual Laws?

We have seen that the universal laws are unbreakable, unchangeable principles of life which operate inevitably all the time for all human beings everywhere. If we think of them, we shall find that they also reveal to us a deep sense of impartiality, equality and fairness. Thus a Universal Law is not like the laws of our Government or like any other man-made laws; it is rather a basic principle of life which explains to us how life works. All of us, therefore, need to know about these vital laws of life which operate under a master *Law of Cause and Effect*, also known as *Karmic Law* (McArthur, 1993; Harra, 2002). The law simply states that *"for every effect there is a cause"* or *"as you sow, so shall you reap."* Thus whatever has happened in our life, we should note that it was not by chance or by bad luck; there was a definite cause behind it. This master law has the following important sub-laws:

1. *Like Begets Like:* We can readily see the application of this law in nature: dogs beget dogs and cats beget cats. If dogs were to beget other creatures at random, there could have been chaos in the Universe. Therefore, this law is basic to our existence. It also operates in our lives and relationships in many important ways and our

attitudes, feelings and actions determine all these also in others (McArthur, 1993):

Our motives beget like motives,
Our emotions beget like emotions,
Our attitudes beget like attitudes,
Our thoughts beget like thoughts,
Our approach begets a like approach,
Our acts beget like acts,
Our spirit begets a like spirit.

2. *The Law of Increase:* We reap abundantly in our gardens and in our lives according to the seeds we sow—not only what we sow, but far, far more—multiplied many times. As we study and observe what takes place in this growth process, we gain a deeper understanding of how the law works in our lives and how we can best work in accordance with it and with the Creative Forces. In short, this law is also known as "As you sow, so shall you reap."
3. *The Law of Attraction:* "Like attracts like" is a law of attraction dealing with the attraction between ourselves and other individuals, things, conditions and places. All of us are familiar with magnets that attract or cling to a piece of steel or to other magnets. Similarly, we, too, have some form of a field around us. Many psychics are able to see this field or aura that exists around human bodies. Charles Fillmore called the field around us as a "thought atmosphere."

   If "like attracts like", there is also a corresponding law of repulsion: opposites repel. For humans, the law of repulsion as well as the law of attraction operates through the fields or auras of individuals.

These two laws raise some questions: What attracts us and what do we attract? What repel us and what do we repel? To answer these questions, we need to be aware that some higher laws are involved which give us the power to bring into our life whatever we choose to seek or repel.

4. *The Law of Balance:* Balance is a state of equilibrium—of health on the physical level, fulfilment on the mental level, and joyousness on the spiritual level. It is an art of handling all aspects of life in a way that results in the greatest good for the person concerned and for others. What we truly seek is a dynamic balance, a condition in which we are attuned and aware, flexible and capable. Then, we can travel the road of life, taking all of it, including its bumps, tough climbs, and sharp curves with understanding, poise, and composure.

   The law of balance is founded on the fundamental nature of the Universe. If we don't make a balanced exchange, the Universe will balance it—at our cost. According to McArthur (1993), there are four broad areas of interchange in our lives: (a) interchanges with our environment, (b) interchanges with others (individuals and groups), (c) interchanges with self (physical, mental, spiritual), and (d) interchanges with the creative forces.

5. *The Law of Manifestation*: One of the most important laws of transformation is the one involving the relationship among the basic elements of our being—sprit, mind, and body. With this law we often create the physical results we see in our lives. It can be diagrammed as follows:

Spirit is the Life, Mind is the Builder and Physical is the Result

Spirit is the beginning of all things in our life; it is also the end of self-development. As souls, we were all Spirit in the beginning, are Spirit plus a body now, and at the end will still be Spirit. It is thus the basis for all the higher Universal Laws of Transformation and Attainment (McArthur, 1993; see Figure 7.1).

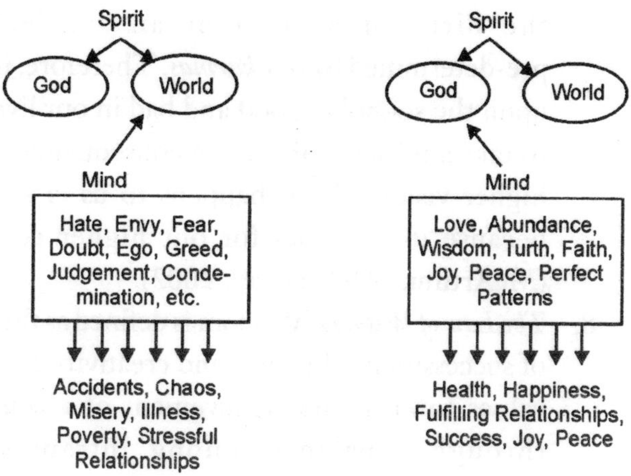

Fig. 7.1: Relationship between Spirit, Mind and Body

6. *The Power of Expectancy*: When we have an attitude of expectancy, our mind senses it and begins to build. Without it, nothing happens. The spirit of expectancy is thus the key that turns on "mind the builder." The degree of expectancy that we maintain is also vital: If we expect much, we get much; if we expect less, we get less, if we expect bad health, we get bad health.

The creative process of this law of expectancy works in accordance with our input. According to McArthur (1993), "it is basically an energy-transforming process." In thinking about negative conditions—past, present or future—we are giving energy to such conditions. Through the creative process, they will grow, expand, and manifest. Therefore, Edgar Cayce has rightly warned that "... do not look for it you will find it."

7. *There is Nothing By Chance*: Many of us believe that, chance, luck, and accidental events play a part in our lives. But this law says that "for every effect there is a cause" and "there are no coincidences." It could be the birth of a child or an accident; all are pre-determined by our *karmas*. Therefore, in reflecting upon the so-called good and bad in our lives, we need to take another look (law of consequences) and seek a higher vision. What happens to us is always Good, because it is always for our higher consciousness (McArthur. 1993; Harra, 2002).
8. *The Law of Wisdom*: Wisdom is defined as the application of successful intelligence and creativity as mediated by values towards the achievement of a common good through a balance among intrapersonal, and extrapersonal interests over short and long terms (Sternberg, 2003). It is knowing about what we can change and what we cannot. It is using our suffering as a way to learn about ourselves and to help others. We shall experience less pain in our life, learn our lessons more peacefully, and prevent and resolve our problems more readily oncc wc gain wisdom. Through wisdom and patience, every karmic issue can be resolved and every person can be helped. Thus, according to Sternberg, wisdom is "value-laden application of tacit knowledge not only for one's own benefit (as can be the case with successful intelligence) but also for the benefit of others, in order to attain a common good. The wise

person realizes that what matters is not just knowledge, or the intellectual skills one applies to this knowledge, but how the knowledge is used."

How Can We Change Our Life?

We have seen that certain spiritual laws govern our lives. Therefore, we need to learn how to make use of these laws from a higher perspective of inner wisdom. For this, we have to keep our minds attuned to the Spirit within. That means, if we wish to change our lives, we must change our choices of pattern. Patterns are chosen from the level of consciousness we hold at the time of making choices. If our life does not change, we need to raise the level of consciousness by following the spiritual laws.

Vedanta says that the power of consciousness is not the built-in-characteristic of the mind. This comes from some higher source known as Soul, *Atman* or Self. Since mind is not the real perceiver or knower of the mental phenomenon, Hindu religion differentiates between the Mind and the Self—the Mind as an object (the known) and the Self as a subject (the knower). Anything that falls into the category of the known does not have consciousness as its very essence whereas the subject or knower does. Thus, there is one ultimate observer or experiencer, and that is the Self and it becomes 'superconscious' mind which helps in choosing the perfect pattern.

Methods of Attunement

A very basic requirement for attunement by any method is some faith that there is a higher power to attune to. This may be known as God or Spirit. Since faith is a soul quality, it certifies that God always lives within and that we can contact His creative force to work in our life. It gives substance to our hopes, and makes us certain of realities we do not see. Therefore, faith is the bridge that spans the gulf between the seen and unseen.

There are many ways in which we can attune to the Spirit. The Cayce readings suggest at least the following seven methods (McArthur,1993):

1. *Prayer*: Prayer is the concerted effort of the physical consciousness to become attuned to the consciousness of the Creator, either collectively or individually. It is about connecting to the divine, recognizing and clearing the karmic events of the day, and speaking out about pains and desires. It is thus talking to God.
2. *Meditation*: Meditation is moving beyond any interfering thoughts and entering a relaxed, attentive, and receptive state of mind. It allows us to be detached from ego and emotions so that we can connect ourselves to God to listen to Him.
3. *Study of Dreams*: Study of dreams helps us in understanding the unconscious mind which holds possibilities which are locked away from the conscious mind. It has at its disposal all subliminal psychic contents, all those things which have been forgotten or overlooked, as well as the wisdom and experience of uncounted centuries which are laid down in its archetypal organs. Dreams reveal all these spiritual and moral possibilities hidden within the unconscious mind.
4. *Service to Others*: Service to others is the greatest service to God. Whenever self is put aside, the spirit is allowed to shine through us. We may feed the poor; we may take care of helpless and needy persons, or perform other endless useful tasks. But all these services must

be given with the right attitude. We should be filled every moment with humble gratitude for the blessing of God for being able to serve others—a kind of feeling of the privilege of serving God indirectly.

5. *Purpose of Life*: The quest for understanding the deeper meaning of life is the turning point in the life of individuals. Vedanta emphasizes that the human form of life is to inquire about the science of absolute truth, God. By this inquiry, *sambandha*, the relationship between the Self and God is established and the pure spiritual knowledge of the Self is understood.
6. *Establishment of Ideals*: Ideal is the principle behind what we think, say and do—the pattern that we use to measure and shape our life. A materialistic ideal is a life pattern based on the desires of the selfish, lower nature. A spiritual ideal, on the other hand, is the highest standard of perfection that we can imagine. It is an unselfish image of what we want to be like, something above and beyond us we want to reach. We, therefore, need to establish spiritual ideals because they can attract blessings and can direct our life.
7. *Law of Guidance*: There are three laws that define how to get the guidance we need in order to deal with any situation in our lives: (a) Seek first the spirit within, and you will find; (b) Ask the spirit with faith, and you will receive; and (c) Knock, with faith in Spirit, and the door will be opened. Every soul's eternal destiny is the kingdom of God—the realization and expression of oneness with the Infinite. No matter who or where we are, we have an inner yearning for His spirit. When we start to give our will to God, the door begins to open to the Holy Spirit.

Conclusion

Regardless of who we are, or where we find ourselves, we have a connection to one another because we are all children of the same God. Deep within us we possess a consciousness of His force, power, love, and presence. That presence is manifested in the world around us by doing the very best that we can. Since the purpose of life is to bring the spiritually of the Creator into the earth, attunement and application are at the heart of spiritual growth. Attunement is the process of reawakening to an awareness of our spiritual nature and our true relationship with God. As mentioned above, the most frequently recommended tools for achieving this attunement are the regular practice of prayer and meditation.

The Universal Spiritual Laws teach us to learn about our own *karma*, how to recognize it, understand its meaning, and fix it if is broken. *Karma* is simply the law cf cause and effect: *as you sow, so shall you reap*. Once we have this realization, it helps us in creating a better life and a state of mind with balance, security, and confidence. Our life is thus a process of resolving karmic issues and moving on. If we don't resolve them everyday, they will accumulate and become bigger. Such accumulated *karma*—accumulated over time and sometimes over many lifetimes—works like the "snowball effect". We, therefore, need to resolve negative *karma* everyday by regular prayer (confession) and by more and more positive acts. Left unresolved, it may never be healed, and we have to live with the consequential suffering. Buddha has rightly said that:

"The wise are those who control their body
who control their tongue
who control their mind
and give up what is before

give up what is behind
give up what is between
So when you go on the other side of existence
if your mind is free
you will not enter again into birth and decay."

References

Harra, C. (2002). *Every day karma*. New York: Ballantine Books.

McArthur, B. (1993). *Your life: Why it is the way it is and what you can do about it.* Virginia, A.R.E. Press.

Powar, C.B. (1997). *Cell Biology*. Mumbai: Himalaya Publishing House.

Singh,T.D. (2004). *Seven Nobel laureates on science and spirituality.* Kolkata: The Bhaktivedanta Institute.

Singh, T.D. (2005). *Life and spiritual evolution.* Kolkata: The Bhaktivedanta Institute.

Sternberg, R.J. (2003). *Wisdom, intelligence, and creativity synthesized.* Cambridge: Cambridge University Press.

Epilogue

This book is about learning to listen to intuition—the voice of Spirit within us—which says that the metaphysical realm is also real. Since we can see the physical realm, touch it, and measure it, many of us believe that only the physical realm is real. Unfortunately, we are limited to only five senses and four observable dimensions (three of space and one of time). Therefore, we do not believe easily in metaphysical realm. Moreover, we cannot scientifically or mathematically prove its existence. But the reality is: it exists and it has a tremendous amount of circumstantial evidences we are all aware of. We, therefore, now need to change our mindset and move forward, away from the hard proof hang-up. Even science itself is in the process of doing so—moving away from the belief that hard proofs are the only type of proof. Is it not a fact that today many of the leading physics geniuses are accepting the Superstring Theory for which there are no "scientific" evidences? And perhaps, there is no chance of ever proving the

Theory scientifically. Likewise, there is a particular Universe theory that some of the leading cosmologists and physicists believe to be a more reasonable theory than the intelligent design theory. With all these in mind, this book has been compiled from various sources to deal with metaphysical realities in psychology and management.

There are seven articles in all in this book—five published in an online magazine, *The Intuitive-Connections Network* published by Atlantic University and two published in Indian journal/book. The first article is the Presidential Address delivered at IIT, Bombay organized by the National Academy of Psychology. This article raises a few basic questions: If psychology is the science of behaviour and mental processes do psychologists understand fully what is mind? what is behaviour? and what is mental process? If not, why? Simply because it has adopted scientific methods which allow psychologists to study only such questions which can be tested in a precise, objective, and publicly verifiable fashion. But what about such aspects of mind and behaviour like faith, trust, confidence, consciousness, spirituality, wisdom, *karma*, etc. which cannot be tested objectively? Watson dropped such words from the subject matter of psychology to make psychology a natural science. But today, we cannot afford to do so and we have to think of a suitable method to study such subject matters. Touching upon all these aspects in details, this paper suggests finally that psychologists need to realize the importance of Intuition as a method of psychology. This will help not only in understanding of the Superconscious or Universal Mind and Effective Behaviour of the human beings but also in verifying the truth obtained through some other methods. When we say that every human behaviour has three facets—the physical, the mental, and the spiritual—how can psychology remain satisfied only with the study of the physical facet?

The second article deals with intelligence, creativity, and wisdom. Many persons have tried to define intelligence but they have not been able to do so fully. Therefore, modern thinking about the nature of intelligence has largely moved beyond the unitary-*versus*-multifaceted issue and is concentrating on how intelligence can be used for success in life. This success, according to Sternberg, depends on: (1) Capitalizing on strengths and correcting or compensating for weaknesses, (2) Adapting to new environment or modifying the environment to suit him or her, and (3) Balancing the analytical, creative, and practical abilities. At the end, however, he finds it difficult to draw anyone additive combination rule of emphasizing analytical, creative, and practical abilities. Therefore, indirectly, he says that success is decided by something else—may be by some divine power. Many belief systems teach that being 'mindful' is the basic principle behind inner peace and contentment which leads to creativity. Being 'mindful' means giving full concentration to whatsoever we are doing in the present, having no real awareness of anything else, becoming completely absorbed, lost in the activity and the moment. Only through such a peaceful mind we can get intuition, creativity, and inspiration because this "extra-ordinary" mind gets the "wisdom". to maintain balance between successful intelligence and creativity.

The third article is a comparison between Eastern and Western approaches to love and spirituality in management. Recently, managers have started showing good interest in integrating spirituality and management because they find this to be very meaningful for their jobs and lives. As a result, they are feeling more concerned towards their employees and are showing 'genuine love' for them. This kind of love is referred to the quality of human existence, personal values and beliefs, interpersonal relationships, and beyond. Since spirituality is also defined as the inner experience of the individual when he/she senses a Beyond, and the ability to create relationships with what are perceived to be Gods and spirits, some managers consider love and spirituality to be the same. But this article differentiates between the two and explains how they play important roles in management. Eastern and Western managers, however, differ in their styles of management of these two. While the Western managers put the whole emphasis on the external factors, the Eastern managers on the internal factors. This article concludes that both these factors are important for good management.

A dream is an illusory activity, particularly of a visual nature, which occurs during sleep. It is essentially a psychological phenomenon with many philosophical, religious and moral implications. The fourth article examines all these and tries to explain how dreams become of prophetic nature in its fourth stage. Everyone will agree that Freud and Jung were the two masterminds in the field of dream analysis. Jung, however, had an edge over Freud because he said that dreams represented the various layers of the mind and contained ineluctable truths, philosophical pronouncements, illusions, wild fantasies, memories, plans, irrational experiences, and telepathic vision. This view is being supported today by many Indian and Western thinkers and researchers. Not only that, they also find that dreams become more and more meaningful from one stage to the other. A good sleep starts with the first stage dream of personal nature including satisfaction of some of the unsatisfied desires of the dreamer. Then, in second stage, the dreamer has a different kind of dream which is more concerned with the information that is beyond his/her awareness. Then, if sleep is uninterrupted, the dreamer experiences third stage dream which is of transformative nature—saying more about solving a difficult problem. Then, when the dreamer's mind is fully (spiritually) prepared, it enters into the fourth and final stage where he/she has prophetic and philanthropic dreams which reflect more about future of the dreamer. Since a person is reaching the Universal Mind only in this stage, it becomes possible for him or to her to glimpse spiritual and moral possibilities hidden in it only in this (fourth) stage.

The fifth article is about universal laws of *karma* and reincarnation. *Karma* is a Sanskrit word which literally means action. But it also signifies cause and effect relationship. Therefore, *karma* has been defined as the mental and physical deeds that determine the effects of our life and rebirth. Since one cannot commit *karma* and expect it to finish with it in one life, there must be many lives to resolve one's *karma*. This is known as reincarnation which postulates that there is a pre-existing soul before birth and continues after death till the soul can arrive finally at one with the Universe. That means, once *karma* is initiated, it must follow three laws until it is spent: (1) Law of Continuation, (2) Law of Consequence, and (3) Law of Compensation. On the universal scale, these are the laws of *karma* and reincarnation which basically state that every action has a reaction and whatsoever we do to others, returns back to us either in this life or in next lives. If one performs pious activities, that will produce good results, but if one is engaged in selfish or sinful activities that will produce bad *karmas* and future sufferings. This follows a person wherever he or she goes in this life or in future lives. And there are no exceptions to these laws for anyone. We, therefore, need to learn about these universal laws of *karma* and reincarnation so that we can cultivate pious activities and spiritual thoughts and can cut the knots of attachment to materialistic life to reach a heavenly realm after death.

The sixth article deals with interpersonal choice and attraction scientifically and spiritually. Interpersonal attraction is the attraction between people which leads to acquaintances, friendships and intimate relationships. It can be viewed as a force acting between two people that tends to draw them together, connect them, and resist their separation. It is a relatively long-term relationship between two or more people based on emotions like love and liking, regular business interactions, or some other type of social commitment. Social psychologists have discovered several factors that help determine which relationships blossom and which ones get nipped in the bud. In general, they find that people are drawn to those who are (1) geographically available; (2) socially "appropriate"; (3) physically appealing; (4) similar or complementary to themselves; and (5) likely to respond in kind. But, apart from these scientific explanations, there are some spiritual explanations as well. They assume that there are souls we have experienced within our past lives, and are experiencing again with them at this time in different bodies. And, every time, we have had a feeling of deep and natural affinity, friendship, love, intimacy, sexuality, and/or compatibility with them. Such persons are known as soul mates because the attractions are at the soul level. This article also differentiates between male energy and female energy and pleads strongly for merging the two to create the sense of completeness. It is just not possible to experience the real romantic and erotic passion without the expression of feminine energy as a woman and masculine energy as a man. A human relationship, however, goes on changing and growing. We, therefore, need to develop every ordinary relationship into a soulmate relationship which is like a beautiful flower. But this does not happen suddenly or by chance; we have to rather work for it.

The seventh article is about how our life is also governed by certain universal spiritual laws. In the last few decades, scientists have unravelled many mysteries behind various life processes, structures and functions of biomolecules. But they have failed to answer the question: what is life? As a result, they have concluded that "life is possibly beyond molecules". This "beyond molecules" is nicely explained by Vedanta, the ancient spiritual science of India, which says that all living beings are animated by presence of a non-chemical or non-molecular fundamental spiritual particle called *atman*. And only due to the presence of *atman*, the body is animated and active, and undergoes six types of transformation: it takes birth, it lives for some time, it grows, it produces offspring, it gradually dwindles, and, at last, vanishes into oblivion. Vedanta adds further that one of the most important characteristics of life which is fundamental of the *atman* is the consciousness and all living beings possess different degrees of consciousness which determine their evolutionary paths. Since consciousness (*cetana*), intelligence (*buddhi*), mind (*manas*) and senses (*indriyas*) are fully developed in a human being; only this form of life is totally equipped to make the deepest inquiry (*jijnasa*)—the spiritual inquiry. This spiritual inquiry reveals that, like physical laws, our life is also governed by certain spiritual laws which are universal in nature and are unbreakable, unchangeable, and inevitable. All these spiritual laws are explained in this article with a view to make use of these laws from a higher perspective of inner wisdom. For this, we have to keep our minds attuned to the Spirit within. Since the purpose of life is to bring the spirituality of the Creator into the earth, finally, we are supposed to learn about attunement with God. And the most frequently recommended tools for achieving this attunement are the regular practice of prayer and meditation.

All these articles thus throw sufficient light on metaphysical realities that exist everywhere and we cannot close our eyes from these realities. It was a mistake on our part that, in the name of science, we had been neglecting these realities. Now, time has come to change our mindset and realize the importance of all these metaphysical realities. This does not mean that we should do it at the cost of physical realities. They are equally important. We, therefore, need to learn to pay equal attention to both the realities—physical and metaphysical. Thomas Kutscher has rightly suggested integrating logic, intuition, and *karma* to lead an effective life. Logic (science) tells us how to make use of our intelligence, reasoning and commonsense to analyze something at the surface level. But this is not sufficient enough to have knowledge and understanding of the issue. For this, we have to take the help of intuitive processes. Self-analysis, quiet time reviews, meditation and prayer take us to the metaphysical realities and establish connection with the *Spirit* within. It is something like connecting into a *Spirit World Internet* which gives us full understanding and Divine guidance. This kind of guidance actually helps us in having such a karmic plan which is always correct and successful. Everyone, therefore, should arrive at his/her karmic plan only through this integration of logic and intuition.

Index